Endorsements for Good Grief

The energy and passion expressed in this book will leave the pages and touch your heart and your soul! I have had the "blessing" of knowing Frank and Leanne for nearly twenty years, and they/he have amazed and humbled me with their absolute commitment to each other — and to their faith!!

Marty Sutter
Founder and Managing Director
Essex Woodlands Health Ventures

One of the least popular pieces of biblical wisdom may be Ecclesiastes 7:2, "Better to spend your time at funerals than at parties." But in Good Grief, *Frank Young has given us a wonderful modern application. This personal, poignant love story is at once a practical guide for dealing with the greatest rupture most of us will face in this life and, at the same time, a wonderful reminder to treasure our spouses in the here and now. Highly recommended reading.*

Hon. John Scott Redd, Vice Admiral, U. S. Navy (Ret.)
First Director, National Counterterrorism Center
First Commander of the US Navy's FIFTH Fleet in the Middle East

Good Grief is a touching testimony to the faith and strength in Dr. Young's fifty-one year relationship with his wife, Leanne, as well as a practical guide to those who are facing and coping with the loss of a loved one.

Anne B. DeMaret
Investor Relations
Essex Woodlands Health Ventures

This is a charming and poignant book on grief that will go directly to your heart. Frank Young's yearning for his wife, Leanne, after her sad death is filled with courage and great love. Intrinsic in his pain is a joy of spirit and deep faith that touches all who dare to understand that death is not the end of love.

One cannot help but feel that even in the depths of grief we can create a way to turn shattering loss into hope and spiritual renewal. Perhaps this, as well, is Love's Final Gift.

Lynn Clapp
Author of Returning Home: A Poetic Journey of Grief and Loss

Frank and Leanne's marriage, with its commitment, deep love, and strong faith was a shining example of a Christian marriage. Frank has now made himself very vulnerable as he shares the raw emotion, grief, and struggles he experienced with Leanne's passing. Good Grief, with its insights and ways to cope spiritually, emotionally, and practically will be a beacon and resource to those who now walk the pathway of being "suddenly single."

Jean Erskine
Executive Assistant to the Senior Pastor
Fourth Presbyterian Church, Bethesda, Maryland

This book apprehends the deep understanding of what people in grief are seeking and feeling: it resonates with clarity and connectedness. Grieving readers may not have the patience or energy to read anything from cover to cover. The elegant utility of Dr. Young's book is providing the reader easy accessibility to poetry, scripture, and practical lessons learned within the same chapter. This is exceptionally helpful for the reader who wishes to go to a subject or style of message directly.

Kevin Tonat, Dr.PH, MPH, (CAPT., USPHS, Ret.)
President, K. Tonat Consulting

Good Grief *is inspiring, touching and heart-warming. It's good for the soul! The book has helped me to appreciate my loved ones around me today, reminds me of the loved ones that I have lost and strengthens my connection to my faith. Frank and Leanne; you are an inspiration to so many (especially me). Thank you for sharing your story and sending such a positive message.*

Paola A. Alvarado
Executive Assistant
Essex Woodlands Health Ventures

GOOD

GRIEF

Love's Final Gift

FRANK E. YOUNG

ELEUTHERA
PUBLICATIONS

Washington, DC • Nassau, Bahamas

Additional copies of this book can be purchased online at:

www.goodgriefbook.info

Address requests for information to:

Eleuthera Publications
455 Massachusetts Avenue, NW#150-144
Washington, DC 20001

publisher@eleutherabooks.com

Front and back cover art created by Martha Malana, MA, ATR-BC, LPC

Interior photos by:
       Tracey Attlee (www.traceyattlee.com)
       Leslie Lane (www.leslielanephotography.com)
       The Young family photo collection

Dedications

To the glory of Jesus Christ, our Lord and Savior, the center of our fifty-one years of married life

To my wife, Leanne, my faithful loving companion, the glue that held our family together

To all those who have become suddenly single and who are struggling with the irreversible loss of a loved one

About the Author

Dr. Frank Young and his late wife, Leanne, have five children, sixteen grandchildren, and one great-grandchild. Frank and Leanne met while Frank was in medical school. They were engaged in June 1956 and wed the following October. Their earthly union lasted over fifty-one years until Leanne's unexpected death in August 2008.

Frank's education included internship and residency in pathology and a Ph.D. from Case Western Reserve University. He is an ordained Presbyterian minister and served as associate pastor at Fourth Presbyterian Church in Bethesda, Maryland. Administrative posts include dean of the School of Medicine and Dentistry and vice president for health affairs at the University of Rochester. He served for five-and-a-half years as commissioner of the U.S. Food and Drug Administration. Frank was a member of the executive board of the World Health Organization and served for twenty years in the U.S. Navy Ready Reserve and the Commissioned Corps of the U.S. Public Health Service, retiring as a rear admiral.

Dr. Young is currently a partner in Essex Woodlands Health Ventures and fulfilling the legacy of love left to him by his beloved Leanne.

Table of Contents

Index of Lessons Learned

Index of Poetry*

*Only poems authored by Dr. Frank E. Young are listed

Acknowledgments

I am indebted to Leanne Young, my companion, friend, lover and supporter, for her many contributions throughout our fifty-one years of marriage. She enabled me to reach my farthest star. In her passage from earth to heaven, she taught me lessons of grace and displayed the deep faith that befits her life verse, Phil. 4:6-7.

I also wish to thank my children, Lorrie, Debora, Peggy, Frank, and Jonathan, for their loving support and encouragement during our journey. Our grandchildren, great-grandchild, and extended family also lightened our burdens during Leanne's illness through their love, care, and laughter in the midst of pain.

Leanne and I were blessed by the preaching and teaching of many pastors, beginning with Dr. John Balyo, who laid the foundation for our spiritual growth and our walk in faith after our marriage in 1956. For the last twenty-five years, we had the privilege of learning from the teaching and preaching of Dr. Rob Norris, senior pastor of Fourth Presbyterian Church. I am particularly indebted to Dr. Norris for the opportunity to serve with him as a pastor.

The women in the intergenerational Bible study and other friends were an integral part of the "circle of care" for Leanne.

I treasure the eight-plus years that I studied together with my friend and colleague Dr. David Allen at monthly luncheons. Thank you, David, for writing the foreword to this book and for your fellowship throughout our time in Washington.

The original paintings for the front and back covers were created by Martha Malana M.A., ATR-BC, LPC, who faithfully designed these commissioned works from my verbal description. Tracey Attlee and Leslie Lane provided skillfully shot photos.

The editorial work of Curt Ashburn contributed immensely to the quality of this book through our technical and philosophical conversations and his thoughtful recommendations.

Finally, I wish to acknowledge the friendship and support of my partners in Essex Woodlands Health Ventures and my partner, Howard Lee, in the Cosmos Alliance. I am grateful for the freedom you gave me to take time off to care for Leanne. I do not know how I could have worked under these circumstances.

Foreword

Dr. Frank Young is a man for all seasons: dean emeritus of the University of Rochester School of Medicine, doctor of philosophy, pastor, and retired rear admiral in the Commissioned Corps of the U.S. Public Health Service. Brilliant, energetic, and compassionate, he has provided guidance and wise counsel in times of trouble to countless persons, including me. His wisdom has blessed the entire nation, but particularly the faithful at Fourth Presbyterian Church in Bethesda, Maryland. But it is impossible to know Frank without recognizing the powerful spiritual presence of Leanne, his wife of fifty-one years.

This is no ordinary book on grief. It is a testimonial of love and faithfulness. Writing as a medical doctor, scientist, pastor, and grieving husband, Dr. Young gives us a glimpse into what is beyond the pain and grief of loss into what the poet Rashani calls the *unbroken* that lies beyond *brokenness*.

The Unbroken

There is a brokenness
Out of which comes the unbroken,
A shatteredness out
Of which blooms the unshatterable,
There is a sorrow
Beyond all grief which leads to joy
And a fragility
Out of whose depths emerges strength.

There is a hollow space
Too vast for words
Through which we pass with each loss,
Out of whose darkness
We are sanctioned into being

There is a cry deeper than all sound
Whose serrated edges cut the heart
As we break open
To the place inside which is unbreakable
And whole,
While learning to sing

—Rashani

Describing himself after losing Leanne, Dr. Young says, "In many ways, this new state of singleness is analogous to a shipwrecked man benevolently tossed upon the shore of a new land." He invites us to work through the anguish and pain of loss and to join him on a journey of faith to a new reality beyond death. "For love is stronger than death and many waters cannot quench it" (Songs 8:6, 7).

Leanne was a saint. Her quiet but powerful spirit blessed us all. Frank and Leanne raised a beautiful family and created an atmosphere of faith, deep love, and oneness. In a changing world where marriage is in crisis, the covenant and commitment between Frank and Leanne is a strong rock of love and faith radiating ripples of hope to a culture in transition. Facing many difficult struggles in their life together which included financial problems, a mentally challenged daughter, and the near-fatal injury of a beloved son, Frank and Leanne journeyed together in faith—walking in victory!

Renewing his marital vows to Leanne in death by writing letters and poems to capture her essence, Dr. Young sends a resounding message of hope in a world of doubt and confusion that "death may destroy a life, but can never destroy a relationship."

This is an important book. It shatters the illusions of modern existence such as chronological fatalism, narcissism, and secular materialism. Dr. Young reminds us that all love is God's love calling us to experience "The love that will never let us go and the face that will never turn away."

Frank and Leanne, thank you for this beautiful legacy of faith, hope, and love, a testimony of life after death for both of you.

Dr. David F. Allen MD, MPH
Distinguished Life Fellow – American Psychiatric Association

Introduction

Suddenly Single

Our stories are the roadmaps of our lives. They reveal and define us. People have been telling stories since they could carve on cave walls and probably earlier. —Edward Grinnin

This book is a chronicle of our journey through the emotional kaleidoscope I experienced after the death of my faithful and loving companion, my dear wife, Leanne. I say *our* journey because she is still my companion. During our fifty-one years of marriage, Leanne enabled me to reach my farthest star through the love, selfless dedication, and nurture that she gave for the well-being of our family. I am deeply indebted to her faith and devotion, which were an integral part of her life. In the three months and eleven days from her diagnosis to her departure for heaven, she gave us many memorable gifts—most of all, the gift of herself.

While I describe the process of spousal grief primarily from a man's perspective, most of the insights apply also to women and to other sources of grief such as the death of a close friend, death of a child, divorce, job loss, or a chronic illness. After so many years of marriage, particularly one characterized by deep intimacy, the loss of one's cherished spouse can throw life into turmoil and lead to a catastrophic downward spiral! Those who love deeply are likely to grieve profoundly. While age might influence the shades of the dark shroud of grief, many common themes emerge during the aftermath of becoming *suddenly single* regardless of the number of years together.

No matter how much time one receives to prepare for the inevitable separation, the passing of one's spouse ushers in an irreversible change in the pattern of living and in emotional stability. I am grateful for one of love's greatest gifts, the final gift of accompanying Leanne to the brink of death, whispering words of comfort to her as she parted. Nevertheless, in spite of knowing for more than three months that I would have to bid her farewell, I felt as *suddenly single* as if I had no warning at all.

As a physician, scientist, and pastor, I had experienced the events surrounding dying first hand. As a pathologist, I had frequent encounters with the dead at the autopsy table. As rear admiral in the Commissioned Corps of the U.S. Public Health Service, I was responsible for coordinating health and medical services for those in crisis in the aftermath of natural and man-made disasters under the Federal Emergency Management Administration through the Federal Response Plan.

The devastating effects of catastrophes such as Hurricane Andrew and the Oklahoma City bombing produced indelible emotional scars on my psyche. Having presided over many memorial and funeral services, I knew the Scriptures of comfort and believed unquestionably in the resurrection of the dead and the promise of everlasting life (John 11). I had been around death all of my professional life, yet none of these experiences prepared me for the emotional devastation of the loss of my beloved wife. Her passing was my own personal catastrophe!

A surviving spouse's search for meaning is a complex one. There are common threads of guilt, purpose, anxiety, questioning, and depression with flashes of relief that the suffering of a loved one is over. While the dominant prevailing mood varies depending on the particular relationship and circumstances, it is widely accepted that the loss of a spouse is one of the greater, if not the greatest, upheaval a person can experience in life.

The title of this book came from my meditations and some free association on the meaning of a common utterance of my granddaughter Sarah. Whenever she encountered the profound, unusual, or mundane in life, she would simply say, "Good grief." I meditated on this phrase after the death of my wife. It is odd that in the catacombs of the mind, one can derive theological meaning from such a common or habitually spoken phrase.

I composed the following poem, "Good Grief," while being led out of the shrouded valley of grief-stricken despair about seven months after my dearest Leanne passed from this world to the next. It captures the dawn of my realization that the incredibly terrible anguish of human grief cannot compare to the grief that God, the Father, suffered upon the death of his only Son. As I rapidly composed the poem from free association, I realized that flickers of light were beginning to appear and were illuminating the darkness of my self-centered despair.

GOOD GRIEF

Is there such a state as good grief?
It is a common utterance, not a belief,
When the fabric of life is torn to shreds,
And your life-long partner is suddenly dead.

The change is indescribably, profoundly sad.
The emotional roller coaster slides from good to bad.
My behavior, motivation, ambition, and joy of life,
Are irrevocably altered with the loss of my dear wife.

Can anything good come from this sorry state?
I know that her pain and suffering will abate.
Immortal until called home is true at last,
And all of us mortals soon must pass.

I have learned as I wander this tortuous path,
That God's Spirit has not led me to wrath.
But instead there are glimmers of brilliant light,
Of hope that someday my spirit will take flight.

My life will never be the same,
It is still raw and racked with pain.
But as I search for purpose anew,
I've discovered a new relationship with You.

God elected some through Jesus to eternal life,
A gift of grace and not the work of our strife,
It cannot be purchased at any price.
For it was bought by our Savior's own dear life.

The pain and grief suffered by Father and Son
Is an immeasurable, incomprehensible victory won.
Jesus suffering the shame of the cross and separations grief,
Conquered death by Good Grief ushering in resurrection belief!

So what does this profound story tell me?
That it is extremely important for me to see
What God's plan is steadily leading me to be
Through the provision of this extra time to me.

So grief is a special personal adventure.
To synthesize a purpose for a new endeavor.
Knitting together the tattered fabric of a bonded life.
Using grief for good by loving God with all my might.

Frank, March 15, 2009

Leanne dying first did not even seem to be in the realm of possibility! Her parents, aunts, and uncles lived into their late eighties and nineties and Leanne had always been in good health. By contrast, my father died of his only coronary occlusion at forty-five, and both of my grandfathers died at fifty-five. Longevity was not in my genes! Haunted by the ghost of my father's early demise, I inflicted the anxiety I had of my early death on my wife and children for years. I always assumed and planned that I would die first. Our children and my wife concurred. I would even comment to our youngest, "I hope I live until you are fourteen so you will remember me." To our older children I would say, "I hope to survive until I meet your fiancées."

With the exception of occasional accidental injuries, my wife was in excellent health until she discovered a little sore on her scalp in 2005. We were concerned and eventually consulted a dermatologist who referred her to a plastic surgeon. The lesion was a superficial melanoma without involvement of sentinel (draining) lymph node with cancer indicating that the malignancy had not spread. The surgeon said that she had a greater than ninety-five percent probability of a cure. In the fall of 2007, Leanne had a severe respiratory infection and I prevailed upon her to obtain a chest X-ray. A small shadow was observed in her lung, but a subsequent CAT scan followed by PET scans and medical consultations concluded that it was probably not a malignancy. While there were shadows of apprehension in our minds, our life returned to its usual state of high activity.

We were preparing for our daughter Lorrie to move in with her sister after living with us for fifty years. Debbie invited Lorrie, who was born with an educational disability, to live in a new addition to her home. Debbie, along with her husband, Richard, and their seven children lived on forty acres on Signal Mountain in Tennessee. This kind offer relieved our greatest concern for the welfare of Lorrie after we were gone. Leanne and I longed for more time together, so I began to decrease my work schedule even as Leanne was gradually developing cognitive symptoms that her doctor diagnosed as depression brought on by Lorrie's move.

We anticipated with great joy our first empty nest and this special time for ourselves. We had begun our family with Lorrie's birth eleven months after our wedding and we had three more children only five-and-a-half years into our marriage. The child rearing fell mostly on Leanne while I completed my internship, residency, and graduate school. Now, after being together for fifty-one years, the dream of having this special time alone disappeared even before Lorrie moved out.

In the chapters that follow, I chronicle our life together and Leanne's journey from this world to the next in my own brand of folksy poetry and prose. The first chapter provides a brief account of our married life, with particular emphasis on our spiritual milestones. This overview will provide the context for our life together after receiving the dreadful diagnosis. Other chapters will focus on the trauma of dealing with an unexpected diagnosis of impending death, the immediate involvement of family and friends, our journey to the final separation, and the wanderings in the aftermath of my beloved's death. A full chapter is dedicated to thoughts on how to grapple with tragedy as a couple experiences the emotional tsunami of a spouse dying. Another chapter provides guidance for wandering on the pathway of grief. The final chapter focuses on considerations for developing the couple's legacy.

Each chapter closes with "Lessons Learned" in the spiritual, emotional, physical, and mental aspects of life. These are discussed from both a general and specific point of view. It is interesting to note that one out of four people will have severe heart disease that results in death, about one in three-and-a-half will have cancer, but one out of one will die leaving his or her loved one in "Grief City." Yet, comparatively little thought and planning is devoted to spousal death and the grief of the *suddenly single*.

I hope these blatantly honest and, at times, vivid stories will aid you in planning for or coping with life's most traumatic experience. I will discuss decisions that couples must confront in dealing with the impending death of a spouse. I will describe the raw wounds and emotional rollercoaster that I experienced in the hope that it will help you, too, grope through the forest of the dark foreboding, mental anguish, and confusion of the soul when you become *suddenly single*.

FEY
April 9, 2011
Bethesda, Maryland

1

Our Married Life in Cameo

For this reason a man will leave his father and mother and be united to his wife and they will become one flesh. The man and his wife were both naked and they felt no shame. —Gen. 2:24-25

Leanne and I met late in February 1956 at Memorial Hospital in Syracuse before I graduated from medical school. Although I knew I would marry her that first night, it took me until the middle of June to persuade her to marry me. Her wholesome family values, honesty, and our mutual faith attracted me deeply. Vigorous and immediate pursuit of this attractive young nurse was imperative, since I was moving to Cleveland to start an internship on July 1 that year. To my everlasting joy, she said, "Yes."

Photo 1: 1956 Leanne during our engagement

On my meager hundred-dollar-a-month internship stipend we could only afford to see each other twice in the three-and-a-half months leading up to our October wedding. Leanne gave me my first assignment during that time: "Find a good church home for us." Our faith continued to grow and bind us tightly together for fifty-one years. Four hours before our wedding I gave Leanne the following poem. It captures well our emotions and commitment to God on the day we exchanged our vows.

THE DAY WE ARE ONE

Today is a day like any day,
And yet it is strange and new,
For in just four short hours,
I'll be going down the aisle with you.

For months we've been drawn together.
Tied and enveloped in the sands of time.
Our thoughts, emotions and ways have blended,
We are almost one in mind.

Seems yesterday, the day we met.
Casually but significant too,
It seemed as if we were drawn together,
You to me and I to you.

Henceforth we will be legally one.
Something we've known for long.
You and I before God and friends today are one!
Our life has begun.
　　　　　　　　　　　Frank, October 20, 1956

Looking back on that wonderful day, I realize we really did not have any big surprises after we were married even though we knew each other for only a few months before our wedding. There were some things Leanne did not know about me like my capacity for hard work. Conversely, I did not know the depth of Leanne's strength in the face of adversity. Our commitment to God was and always remained the bedrock of our marriage. We were madly in love and devoted to each other no matter what! We embarked on many adventures that enabled us to become one "LeanneFrank". We bonded for life!

Photo 2: October 20, 1956

Cleveland

After a magical wedding on October 20, 1956, we began our married life in Cleveland. Due to our prolonged separation, Leanne began her married life with a virtual stranger, in an unknown city, working in an unfamiliar hospital.

We assumed that becoming pregnant would be difficult so we thought we better get started trying just two months after getting married. We were wrong, conception occurred rapidly and Leanne was soon pregnant with Lorrie. To make ends meet, we left our attic apartment in a two-story home in Cleveland Heights and moved to an inner-city housing project before Lorrie's birth.

Although Leanne suspected that Lorrie had a developmental problem, we learned only later that the severe jaundice in her first three days of life was due to an ABO blood incompatibility. Six years after her birth, we received the correct diagnosis that Lorrie was educationally handicapped. This was the first crisis of our married life. She would be highly functioning, but would require continual special education. Lorrie would live with us for fifty years. The sad truth is that a simple blood transfusion would have prevented Lorrie's disability.

Midway through the first year of internship, we prayed about whether I should seek a Ph.D. in the pathology training program. Through God's providence, I was accepted as a graduate student in the department of microbiology. We were as poor as church mice, but madly in love. Leanne managed our meager resources and raised the children while I completed my internship, residency, and a doctorate in microbiology.

Photo 3: Leanne, Lorrie, and Debbie

Leanne put her skills as an assistant head nurse to good use in our household. Later, I queried, "How did you survive in our rented two-bedroom apartment with four children and essentially no help from me?" She coyly replied, "It was sink or swim and I decided to swim."

Seven years after our wedding, I was awarded my Ph.D. from CWRU (Case Western Reserve University) and immediately went to work as an assistant professor of pathology. Meanwhile, Leanne had squirreled away some money which, supplemented by a second mortgage from the department of pathology, enabled us to make a down payment on our fixer-upper home. Most importantly, we developed a deeper foundation in faith and practical Christian living through our church's Young Married Class and under the sound biblical teaching of Rev. John Balyo.

I began a career in academic pathology by setting up a laboratory within the lab complex of another professor, Dr. Irving Lepow, while at the same time applying for research grants. Leanne managed our home and raised the children enabling me to work vigorously to establish my academic abilities. The research and teaching progressed rapidly and I was considered for the position of professor and chairman of the Department of Pathology at CWRU. After much praying over a list of pros and cons as suggested by Pastor Balyo, we decided to accept an associate professorship in microbiology and experimental pathology at Scripps Clinic and Research Foundation in La Jolla, California. We had concluded that at the age of thirty-three, I was not prepared to be a department chairman.

The hope of good schooling for Lorrie, and a better climate for our youngest son, Frank, who was afflicted with bronchitis, proved irresistible. The opportunity to build my own laboratory and to do full-time research, unencumbered with administrative or teaching duties, was an added bonus. So we gathered our four children and my mother in our station wagon and set off with mixed feelings of regret at leaving our church home and moving 3,000 miles from our parents. We were going west on a great adventure!

La Jolla

Our five years in the golden West were a remarkable break from our earlier arduous struggles. We were able to purchase a nice four-bedroom, ranch-style home in La Jolla just three blocks from UCSD (University of California at San Diego). Leanne was elated as I carried her over the threshold into our new home in 1965. This was the first time that she ever saw the house that she trusted me to purchase. She was surprised as she darted from room to room examining our completely furnished home. The furniture was far better than anything we had ever owned! I had purchased all of the furniture from the previous owners and augmented it with a few pieces from a discount store to replace our shabby hand-me-down furniture. Leanne described our sojourn in

California as five years of vacation. Our home was a few miles from the beach. The Scripps Clinic and Research Foundation was right on the ocean and, best of all, there was no snow.

Our family enjoyed idyllic hours on the beach, camping in Sequoia and Yosemite national parks and taking trips to the surrounding desert and mountains. We lived in a nice community and the lighter work schedule provided an opportunity to enjoy our four small children. Our parents made extended visits and we also took a cross-country trip back east to visit them. These prolonged travels provided fun times and enabled us to see much of the country by taking different routes to and from California during each trip. In retrospect, this was the most trouble-free time of our marriage. Near the end of our delightful five years in California, God blessed us with our fifth child, Jonathan. His was an unexpected pregnancy, hence his name which means "gift of God." We were surprised, but delighted. Now our family was complete.

Our spiritual life was strengthened through Sunday school and church. Pastor Allen Smythe involved me in teaching Sunday school for the first time and mentored me in sharing my faith, but although we were active in our Christian community, we continued as covert Christians in the secular world.

Two particular events served to strengthen our walk with Christ. First, I agreed to debate a pastor of a church that we briefly attended before we realized that he did not believe in the validity of the resurrection of Jesus. In this Good Friday debate, I posited the bodily resurrection of Jesus while the pastor expressed his doubts. Little did I know that the religion reporter for the San Diego Union was in the audience. To my great surprise, the Saturday paper gave the debate extensive coverage—I was outed!

Now my colleagues at the University of California and Scripps Clinic knew of our beliefs. Until that time, I had successfully hidden my faith except when I was in the Christian community. I now embarked on informal Christian teaching and lay preaching. Leanne was my constant encourager and supporter in these activities. Later, we became advisers to the student IVCF (InterVarsity Christian Fellowship) at the UCSD. They met in our home, which was located close to the university. The second challenge arose in connection with the mentoring of students. The members of the InterVarsity Fellowship were in a very secular environment where peers and professors challenged and often ridiculed their faith. This was particularly true in the department of history in which professor Herbert Marcuse expounded an atheistic theology.

I learned in a publication that professor John Montgomery had debated Professor Marcuse at a conference. Leanne and I reasoned that it would be great to have him on campus as a counterweight in the department of history, the area of Dr. Montgomery's doctorates. After all, the very word *university* embodies the concept of a balanced representation of many views. Accordingly, I made an appointment to explore a sabbatical for Dr. Montgomery with the provost of UCSD where I was an adjunct associate professor.

The provost informed me that he would like to have him on campus, but that there were insufficient funds. My response was to take out my checkbook and write a check for Dr. Montgomery's sabbatical salary even though there were not enough funds in our account to cover the debit. Later that day, I called John Alexander, President of InterVarsity. After explaining the dialogue with the provost, I asked John if he could advance me the funds in the full confidence that we could repay the money through offerings from the lectures that John was willing to give in the San Diego area. By the end of the semester, the funds were available to repay InterVarsity. It was the first time that we learned to walk by faith, a lesson that would last throughout our married life.

We moved from La Jolla to Rochester, N.Y., because of a conditioned prayer. In 1969, the universities were under attack. Students were rebelling against authoritarian institutions and a nagging question reverberated in my mind: Was it appropriate to continue to exist in a sheltered research institute or should I go back to the academic headwaters from which I sprang? Leanne and I discussed and prayed about this question. Finally, we decided to undertake a Gideon-like approach. I was eligible for a lifetime salary award for research from the American Cancer Society. I applied for it as a test. We prayed that if I was to stay at Scripps, I would be awarded the grant; if not, we prayed that I would be given a sign indicating God's will for our future.

The chairman of the department of microbiology, where I was a professor, was on the award committee. He, of course, had to recuse himself from the decision. On the Friday after the meeting, he told me that the application was approved, but he did not know whether the score was sufficiently high to be funded. In the next five working days, I had four offers to be considered as chairman of either a department of pathology or microbiology. I had received occasional letters before, but never in such a flurry. Leanne and I concluded it was the answer to our prayers and we committed to interview for each position. The University of Rochester appeared to be the logical choice based on comments from Dean Orbison about the role of faith in medicine and the educational advantages for Lorrie. We moved back to snow country five years to the day after we had arrived in sunny southern California.

Rochester

Our relocation to Rochester was good, but difficult. We drove across country as a family, but I had to return to Scripps to pack up the laboratory. Leanne and the children remained in Rochester without me for about a month living in another faculty member's home. In addition to caring for the children in a strange city, she had to select the remaining fixtures for our new home. I never realized how difficult this task was for her as I was preoccupied with moving my laboratory equipment, supplies, five postdoctoral students, and a graduate student. A lack of mutual understanding of each other's problems further complicated our first few pressure-packed months.

I assumed the leadership of a department of microbiology that was overcoming the turmoil of a traumatic resignation of the former chairman from his administrative position. I also had to revitalize both the teaching and research programs. Leanne was coping simultaneously with our newborn infant, four other children, and managing our home. We really did not understand or support each other. One evening, Leanne stormed into my study and stated emphatically that we were not compatible. I shot back, "Do you want a divorce!" Leanne's tears flowed profusely and we began to talk about our problems. We uncorked our roaring emotions and reconciled. Thus, we resolved our only major marital confrontation. Yes, there were other skirmishes, but none were ever of this magnitude.

Our neighborhood in Rochester was ideal for our family's development. We lived near other families with children and snowy winters provided outdoor recreation as well as a natural confinement that fostered family interaction. One day, on the way to church, we saw an ox yoke in an antique shop. We bought it and hung it on our fireplace as the symbol of our marriage and to teach our children the importance of being equally yoked in marriage.

We also shared our faith beyond the family. Leanne started a neighborhood Bible study and we were active in church through my Sunday school teaching. At the university we helped organize a branch of the Christian Medical Society. An interesting dynamic ensued when I co-taught a course entitled "Origin of the Universe and Emergence of Life" on the undergraduate campus with an associate professor in the department of religious studies. We discussed the beginnings of the universe, evolution, and creation, but we did not reveal our inner convictions. At a dinner in our home at the end of the course, the forty-eight students were surprised to learn that the professor of religious studies was an agnostic and the scientist was an evangelical. A vigorous discussion ensued!

My research prospered and the laboratory grew to pre-eminence both in the medical school and nationally. I was also involved in clinical microbiology and eventually became a clinical chief at Strong Memorial Hospital. Life was good! Subsequently, I became dean of the School of Medicine and Dentistry and later vice president for health affairs as well. This was the toughest job of my academic career and, unfortunately, it came during the teenage years of our four children. Leanne continued to be the dominant nurturer of our family. After five years in the deanship, and through the extraordinary effort by many people, the hospital was salvaged from debt, numerous chairmen were recruited, and Leanne and I learned to balance the social and community responsibilities of the position.

During my tenure as dean, I continued laboratory research in biotechnology and participated in policy deliberations on the regulation of recombinant DNA as a charter member of the NIH (National Institutes of Health) Recombinant DNA Advisory Committee. To my surprise, a unique opportunity arose to go to Washington as commissioner of the FDA (U.S. Food and Drug Administration) and to initiate the process of the national and international regulation of the biotechnology revolution. Since my research was in genetic engineering and biotechnology, the challenge proved to be irresistible.

We shed many tears because we had just redecorated our home in preparation for a fund raising campaign for the School of Medicine and Dentistry. Although Leanne embraced the move, I felt as if I had again forcibly transplanted a thriving bush to rocky soil in a new and, this time, an intensely political environment.

About the time we left Rochester for our new home in Bethesda, Maryland, a suburb of Washington, D.C., our children were making lives of their own. Our daughter Peggy married Nathan Long, the son of a missionary to Vietnam. Our daughter Debbie was a missionary for Young Life in Baton Rouge, Louisiana, and our son Frank was soon to be married. I departed Rochester alone and was sworn in on July 15, 1984. In the meantime, Leanne packed up our home. Our church commissioned us in September for service in Washington and we set off for our new home with Lorrie and Jonathan.

Washington, D.C.

Rather than describe our twenty-four years in the Washington scene, a few spiritual, family, and emotional highlights will serve better to help you understand our partnership and walk of faith. The location of our home was a tremendous answer to prayer. First, it was within a half-mile of Jonathan's high school and Lorrie was able to take the bus from a stop just three houses down from our home to her job in the cafeteria at NIH. Second, we attended Fourth Presbyterian Church, which was only about three miles away. We struggled to adapt to our new surroundings and adjust to a sub-cabinet position in the Reagan administration. It was an intense political environment and a big change in responsibilities.

Leanne and I became "wrestling parents" when Jonathan followed his older brother's example and became a very talented wrestler. We reveled in his growing expertise. Whenever possible, we went to the wrestling matches and, as a physician, I was glad to be there to help in case an injury occurred.

When Jonathan had a match on the same night as a White House Christmas reception, we chose to attend his match. At the time, we had no way of knowing that Jon would suffer a life-changing tragedy that very night. In the course of his match, he was attempting a pinning throw, but was unable to complete it properly. The move required him to have his arms around his opponent which prevented him from breaking his fall. He struck his forehead full force on the mat. Providentially, he fell out of bounds which stopped the match. He was immediately motionless!

I rushed to the mat and did a quick neurological examination. He was obviously a paralyzed quadriplegic. I cut off his headgear and waited for what seemed like an eternity for an ambulance to arrive. I pleaded with them to take him to the National Naval Medical Center in Bethesda or a comparable comprehensive trauma center. They refused and took him by ambulance to the nearest facility, Montgomery General Hospital. As I suspected, they could not manage such a trauma case so I refused to let them admit him. Instead, I insisted they summon a helicopter to transfer him to a comprehensive trauma center. The MedSTAR helicopter arrived and the medical crew saved his life en route to Washington Hospital Center by shocking him twice to restore cardiac function. Jon later informed us that he remembered them saying, "We're losing him!"

Meanwhile, we were driving in a state of shock to the hospital. We could hardly pray, but one of us uttered the words, "Lord, we have one child with a strong body and a weak mind and another with a paralyzed body and a strong mind. Please, just let him live. We will manage somehow." When we arrived at the hospital, the doctors told us he would survive. He would probably have some arm movement and any movement of his hands would be "icing on the cake." However, he would never walk again!

We were devastated, but by the grace of God, an outstanding neurosurgeon was on call that night. There was a race to get his spinal column aligned within three hours to prevent extensive loss of blood flow to his spinal cord. I accompanied Jonathan to the CAT scan and watched his spinal cord come up slice by slice. Praise God, there were no bone fragments or hemorrhages in his spinal cord. Dr. Dennis had previously inserted screws in his head and successfully realigned his vertebra to reduce the compression of Jon's spinal cord. Now Jonathan could be transported to the ICU (Intensive Care Unit).

Leanne and I took turns staying in the chair next to his bed in the ICU. We observed his erratic pulse and respirations in utter fear. We notified his brother Frank and sisters, Lorrie, Debbie, and Peggy. Debbie and Peggy, both about six months pregnant, traveled to Washington to be of assistance. The staff in the ICU successfully stabilized Jonathan and then transferred him to a room on a rocking bed to prevent bedsores until he could undergo surgery. Since Leanne and two of our daughters were nurses, one of us could stay with him every night. Nights were always busy because Jon would alternately ask us to take off his covers, pull up his covers, scratch his nose, rub his face, massage his scalp, etc. Understandably, Jonathan was very uncomfortable in the rocking bed and needed constant attention. He slept fitfully.

Four events are seared into my mind regarding his injury and hospitalization that I can only attribute to God's providence. First, immediately after his injury, Jonathan had an out of body experience. He successfully described his exact position on the mat. He said he saw himself on the mat from above and that he went through a tunnel to a bright light where there were people ready to greet him. Then, he looked down and saw me kneeling next to him in the gym. Jonathan stated that he did not want to die in his father's arms so he fought back. I was amazed at these incredible descriptions.

Second, I stayed with Jon in the hospital the night Pastor Norris and some of the elders came in to anoint him with oil. They read Isaiah 40:30-31.

> Even the youths grow tired and weary and young men stumble and fall; but those who hope in the Lord will renew their strength. They will soar on wings like eagles; they will run and not grow weary, they will walk and not faint.

After they anointed him and prayed, Jon rested so peacefully that I kept getting up to listen to his breathing. In fact, his sleep was so peaceful that I feared he might be dead. The next day, when the nurse checked his vital signs, Jonathan told her exactly what his pulse, respirations, and blood pressure were. I had never seen that before.

Third, about thirty years ago, when I was at CWRU as a young assistant professor, I had a group of six students who I tutored at night once a week as a special elective in pathology. To my great comfort, one of them was now the CEO of Washington Hospital Center. Jonathan received excellent care and Leanne and I were able to stay with him during the entire day. At that time, I was still commissioner of the FDA and kept in touch with work from an office near his bed. My Deputy, John Norris, was able to implement my decisions.

Fourth, Leanne was crying in bed one night and, unbeknownst to me, went downstairs and out onto the porch. While sobbing, she read the Epistle to the Philippians. In prayer, she asked God to make Jon whole from his paralysis. She heard God say, "He is whole, but in a new way." Only later, did we realize Jonathan's injury would redirect his life in an unusual way. Eventually, Jonathan completed a PhD in history at the University of North Carolina at Chapel Hill. His thesis was on the Americans with Disability Act. Subsequently, he obtained a position in the Clinton White House in the Office of Public Liaison dealing with the disability community.

After his political position, Jonathan attended and graduated from Yale Law School. He married a lovely woman, Nellie Wild, who was also working in the disability community. We enjoyed having them and their three children living within four miles of us. Later, Jonathan continued in politics in a part time position as the chairman of the National Council on Disabilities in the Obama administration.

It gives me great joy to tell you about Jonathan's life today. His spinal cord injury proved to be incomplete. While he has functional limitations due to partial paralysis, he regained the ability to walk and has gone on to live a full life, which includes advocacy for people with disabilities.

In contrast to Jonathan, who was now weak in body, our daughter Lorrie was physically healthy, but she had a learning disability. Lorrie had a wonderful job working in the cafeteria at NIH. She was trained for this vocation at the special public school in Rochester. She commuted to work by bus and labored in a very safe environment for over twenty years. We were extremely proud of her because she used her intellectual capabilities to their fullest extent and she was emotionally well-adjusted. Lorrie's excellent adjustment to her disability was due to Leanne's nurturing over the years. Leanne continued to help Lorrie mature and exercise independence while still living at home.

Leanne married a very busy man. My responsibilities at FDA were extraordinarily demanding and, once again, this meant that we had to divide our responsibilities into well-defined roles. She skillfully and efficiently managed all household activities including the maintenance on our home and our family's financial security through the careful stewardship.

Leanne also had a number of additional social responsibilities related to my government appointment that stretched both of us in new ways. We joined the Fourth Presbyterian Church in Bethesda, Maryland where we became active in the Sunday school program. She was involved in numerous Christian organizations. Leanne developed her ministry primarily as a one-on-one mentor and counselor of women. She also started an intergenerational Bible study for older and younger women that met in our home. She was a valued mentor for young women for the seventeen years prior to her death. She also had a broader outreach to the congregation as a pastor's wife.

Meanwhile, I spent almost six years in the vortex of controversy at FDA dealing with the implementation of the ten-point action plan to renew the agency. I was involved in domestic issues such as the AIDS crisis, food safety, managing numerous tampering incidents, implementing medical device legislation, presiding over the generic drug crisis, and participating in the continuity of government program. My international involvements included activities at the OECD (Organization of Economic Cooperation and Development) in Paris, WHO (World Health Organization), and the Economic Forum in Davos, Switzerland.,

After I left FDA, I was appointed deputy assistant secretary for health, science, and environment with staff coordination of CDC (Centers for Disease Control), NIH, and environmental health programs in the Office of the Assistant Secretary for Health within the Public Health Service in the DHHS (Department of Health and Human Services). In spite of its complex description, this was the easiest post in more than twelve years of government service. It was a much needed respite for both of us from the hectic pace of my work at the FDA.

Subsequently, I accepted an appointment in the Clinton administration as director of the office of emergency preparedness in DHHS and also as director of the national disaster medical system. Thus, I was heavily involved in responding to natural and man-made disasters through the coordination of the health and medical or emergency support function of FEMA

Upon my retirement from government, our lives changed unexpectedly in a major way. By God's providence, I became director of adult education at Fourth Presbyterian Church and, subsequently, became an ordained minister in the Evangelical Presbyterian Church denomination. I served for over six years as pastor for adult ministries and executive director and ultimately the vice president for the Metro Washington/Baltimore extension of Reformed Theological Seminary. One of my responsibilities was to seek an endowment for the seminary. To that end, I underwent another metamorphosis by venturing into business in my initial field of biotechnology to seek contributions for the endowment.

All of these changes brought with them new responsibilities and rapid spiritual growth. Throughout it all, Leanne and I prayed together and mutually sought God's leading for our lives. In our minds, we were always on spiritual deployment.

In the spring of 2000, I began to experience chest pain on exertion. After a stress test and coronary artery catheterization, the cardiologist said that I must remain in the hospital and have immediate bypass surgery the next morning. He informed me that the anterior descending coronary was completely obstructed and the current symptoms were due to a closure of the right coronary artery. I needed emergency surgery to replace an extensively diseased right coronary artery and, if possible, the left circumflex coronary branch.

Based on my family history, I knew that there was a high probability that I would not survive the surgery. There was also a significant possibility of cognitive impairment due to the heart-lung machine necessary to oxygenate the blood. God was gracious, thanks to lots of prayer and Leanne's nursing, I regained my strength.

The celebration of our fiftieth wedding anniversary on October 20, 2006 was a highlight of our time in Washington. Because of my family history of cardiovascular disease, reaching this unexpected milestone was a special gift. Little did we know that Leanne probably had metastases in her brain at that time. We would only celebrate one more anniversary together! Now that I am "suddenly single", photo four and photo five are comforting reminders of that beautiful celebration. On the occasion of the first anniversary after Leanne's passing, I wrote the poem "Forever" as I clearly realized that we were still united though physically separated.

FOREVER

It was a day of fall splendor,
With colored leaves, cool balmy weather,
When you gave me your heart so young and tender,
And entrusted this treasure to me then and forever.

As years passed in rapid measure,
You secured our homes with care so tender,
I never doubted the safety and security of all your endeavors,
As you poured yourself into each one of your charges forever.

When serious troubles emerged as they often do,
We saw them together through and through,
Joy mingled with pain was accepted without skipping an endeavor
By avoiding self-reliance and abiding in God's grace forever.

Now in the winter of our lives blessed with memories we treasure,
We are apart for a season of unknown length and measure,
But united as two hearts tightly bound and still beating together,
As we look to our love through eternity with our Savior forever.
                                        —Frank, October 20, 2008

Photo 4: Jonathan, Peggy, Lorrie, Leanne, Frank, Debbie, Frank IV

Photo 5: Leanne and Frank's 50th Anniversary

Lessons Learned

1. First, Christ needed to be central in our bonded marriage. During our courtship, we committed to each other that our relationship with Jesus would be the most important part of everything we would do together.

2. We learned that there were three concepts, each beginning with the letter *C*, which defined how we wanted to relate to each other. The first *C* was commitment. We needed to be unequivocally committed to forming a hedge of fidelity around our marriage "...until death do us part." Leanne and I would be united in a Christ centered marriage inside this hedge.

   The second *C* was conflict resolution. A couple gets to know each other intimately through conflict resolution, not through the silent treatment or anger. We agreed to strive to understand each other and, in particular, the stress that the other experienced. When we got into difficulty, it was primarily due to the inability to resolve real or imagined conflicts.

   The third *C* was communication. From the beginning, we did our best to communicate our innermost feelings to each other. We were best friends as well as lovers and parents. We worked at communicating our love for each other in many ways during our fifty-one years of marriage.

3. Trust is an essential ingredient in any marriage. Trust takes years to refine and can be broken through a single indiscretion. We were fortunate to have a deep trust and empathy for each other. We actively worked to cultivate these two traits. They enabled us to address crises with confidence and respect for each other. Because we believed we had each other's best interests at heart, we were able reach difficult decisions. By no means do I wish to imply that there were not times of conflict and disappointment. There were! However, these tools gave us the ability to work through a variety of challenges.

4. We learned that at critical junctions we must pray for guidance. This was in addition to our regular daily prayer life and might take the form of praying over lists or conditioned prayer. We sought to find God's will for our lives.

I must hasten to add that our life was not trouble-free or idyllic. Throughout our fifty-one years of marriage, we dealt with the heartbreak of having a child with an educational disability because of the failure of doctors to diagnose a new syndrome, the devastation of a son who was suddenly rendered a quadriplegic, the shared pain of our oldest son's separation from his wife, and my bypass surgery.

Finally, we had to cope spiritually and emotionally with the activities of my very busy professional life. In our later years, we were able to have almost daily devotions with Bible study, prayer, and hymn singing. I cherish the memories of these devotions now that we are apart!

5. We learned that the only constant in marriage is change. Financial limitations, modification of family life accompanying the growth and marriage of children, translocations resulting from different jobs, illnesses, death of loved ones, and the pressures of competing activities of work, family, church, and personal time required adaptation.

6. Throughout our married life, we experienced the emotional turmoil that accompanies the kinds of trauma listed in lesson four above. The disasters where I assisted people in great anguish, such as the Oklahoma City bombing, Hurricane Andrew and the mid-west flood produced grief as I watched people cope first hand with loss and death of loved ones. These emotional components and spiritual challenges presenting as signs and symptoms of grief were not as intense as those that I was to experience with Leanne's death. Nevertheless, indelible trauma was etched upon my mind. It is clear that people responding to mass casualties, whether they are related to domestic events, natural disasters, or war, can exhibit many of the same signs and symptoms of grief. Even positive events such as our various moves from one city to the next had an element of loss as we grieved leaving friends and colleagues.

Grief is a universal human emotion and the death of a spouse is the ultimate wrenching and tearing apart of the fabric of life. It is a profound irreversible loss!

2

Events Leading to the Dreadful Diagnosis

*We just keep losing things: wives, husbands, friends, health, the dreams
and security of the past. Nothing stays the way it was.* —C. Craig Barnes

Each of us has unique ways of coping with illnesses. I am a
hypochondriac. Leanne was stoic in the face of minor or major
illnesses. That is why I did not know about the sore on Leanne's
scalp until about a month after its appearance. At our family's
urging, Leanne consulted a dermatologist who reassured her that
it was likely only a seborrheic keratosis. Nevertheless, she took a
shaving and sent it to pathology. Two weeks later, we learned that
it was a superficial melanoma. A plastic surgeon removed that as
well as the sentinel lymph node, which is the primary drainage for
that region of the scalp.

Because the lymph node was negative and the melanoma was
superficial, the surgeon told us that she had a ninety-five percent
probability of a cure. We were extremely grateful for this good
news. Then, in the fall of 2007, Leanne developed a severe upper
respiratory infection. A chest X-ray revealed a shadow thought to
be benign. By early 2008, she began to show symptoms that her
primary care physician attributed to depression related to Lorrie's
impending move to Tennessee to live with her sister Debbie.

In February 2008, I had a vision that Leanne would precede
me in death. We had always assumed that I would die first
because Leanne's parents lived into their nineties and I had a
poorer family health history. My father died of a sudden coronary
occlusion at forty-five and my grandfather died of a heart attack at
fifty-five. On top of all of that, I had bypass surgery in 2000. I had
also experienced an asymptotic heart attack in the past.

Nevertheless, because of the vision, I suggested that we
update our files and records. I saw no reason for Leanne to carry
my haunting specter of an early death and we continued to live as
usual. Of course, we did all of this not expecting that Leanne had a
disease that was spreading undetected.

In retrospect, we saw, but did not appreciate, some cognitive changes. For instance, when I was away on an overnight business trip in early April 2008, Leanne was unable to give my brother directions to a freeway that we traveled frequently. When I arrived home from the overnight trip, I was unaware of these symptoms. Leanne, true to form, did not wish to worry me while I was away. Unaware of the looming devastation, I began to prepare a three-day celebration for her seventy-seventh birthday. The first gift was a lovely white orchid and a simple poem.

My Dearest Darling: Thank You for the Gift of You

So many years ago, I found you,
My only love so true,
Through years of devotion,
You blessed me with the gift of you.

Now the twilight approaches us,
But your faithful love shines true.
You are wife, mother, and grandma
But above all—it is the gift of you.
Frank, April 6, 2008

Upon reading the poem and receiving the gift, Leanne burst into tears and blurted out, "Something is dreadfully wrong." She said that she did not know how to drive back from the women's retreat (over a hundred miles away) and was very scared while driving. To this day, I do not know how she found her way. Leanne never drove again. After a medical history, a physical exam, and laboratory work, her primary care physician confirmed his original diagnosis of depression.

We got a second opinion from a psychiatrist who recommended a CAT scan after listening to Leanne describe her symptoms. I vividly remember the doctor saying, "I am ninety-nine percent sure that I will call you in the morning and inform you that nothing is wrong." We were reassured and scheduled a CAT scan on April 23 at noon. It was a simple procedure and Leanne returned to the waiting room after a few minutes.

The technician informed us that she needed to obtain an opinion from the radiologist as to the quality of the film. We became increasingly apprehensive as the minutes passed in slow motion. We held hands tightly as Leanne sobbed gently. After what seemed to be an eternity, the radiologist came in and said without emotion, "You have fourteen tumors in your brain and you need to go to another radiology facility for a higher resolution scan. Our instrument is temporarily out of service." He left abruptly as we sat devastated and cried in each other's arms with wrenching sobs. Eventually, we began to process the heart-breaking news. We vowed to face whatever came our way by relying on God and walking hand-in-hand and heart-in-heart. Over the next four months, we would learn the immensity of that commitment.

As an aside, the radiologist who confronted us in such a matter-of-fact fashion with this devastating diagnosis confirmed the reputation of his profession. Excellent physician/patient interpersonal skills are essential! His behavior was disturbing to me on both a professional and personal level. When I was the dean of the School of Medicine and Dentistry at the University of Rochester, I repeatedly emphasized to the medical students that it was imperative to be compassionate when delivering the diagnosis of a life-threatening condition. This is just a matter of common human decency.

Drs. John Romano and George Engle pioneered this approach to bio-psycho-social medicine. Compassion is especially important in emergency medicine where physicians often treat people with life-threatening conditions. The emphasis needs to be on the well-being of the whole person at the time of the emergency, *not merely the diagnosis!*

We prayed as best we could as we drove in shock to the next diagnostic facility. I do not remember anything about the drive as we struggled to process Leanne's death sentence. Following the second procedure, we somehow managed to navigate the car home. We relayed the diagnosis first to our daughter Debbie, then our daughter-in-law, Nellie, and finally, to the rest of the family. We asked each to pray for us to be strong and of good courage.

Then, before my eyes, *I observed Leanne transform from a sobbing wife to a person of resolute steel.* She smiled at all of us and told me that we would face this together. She said that no matter what happens, "God's will be done." I was amazed! I had observed her inner strength before, but this was a remarkable display of faith and courage.

The First Forty-Eight Hours

The most important first step in coping with a life-threatening disease involves processing the magnitude of crisis and carefully determining the strategy for coping with it. While the dynamics will vary with family relationships, faith, age, the initial prognosis, as well as the seriousness of the disease, the overall steps that a couple must take are roughly the same. First, the person receiving the diagnosis will have varying degrees of denial in the initial stage of coping. This is usually followed by some degree of anger.

It is critical to inform close relatives and friends in a timely fashion. Internalizing the burden of impending death while in a state of shock is usually too heavy to bear alone. In my experience as a physician and a pastor, I have all too frequently seen people attempt to hold the dreadful diagnosis inside. Instinctively, we decided to inform each of our children directly and rapidly. Leanne had followed the same process when I needed emergency bypass surgery and when we notified the family after Jonathan's sudden quadriplegia. If the couple is too distraught, another member of the family or their pastor can assist in this difficult task.

Such communication begins a "circle of care" that will likely last the duration of the illness and beyond. Eventually, the "circle of care" will assume various responsibilities depending on each one's skill and family delegation. It is imperative to follow one principle in particular during the initial phase of the crisis: Do not take over the management of care without permission. *Be sure to maintain the dignity of the one with the life-threatening illness.*

In the immediate aftermath of such a devastating diagnosis, there is usually emotional volatility associated with potential guilt and even hostility toward the person with the life-threatening disease. Be prepared! People will have different primary concerns and priorities. Young children will worry about how the disease of a parent will affect them personally. Adult children and siblings may have unresolved conflicts that will catapult to the fore. A spouse may suffer from guilt, separation anxiety, and fears of financial crises. You must minimize guilt associated with the event. Recognize that everyone will be emotionally fragile in the immediate aftermath of a serious diagnosis. Expect a kaleidoscope of emotions within the inner circle of relationships. Avoid going off half-cocked and err on the side of grace.

After we called all family members and informed them of the unexpected diagnosis of Leanne's brain cancer, I set about trying to get opinions concerning the available options. Within the first twenty-four hours, I did my best to write a chronology of events and the diagnostic tests Leanne had undergone. Then I contacted a number of my physician colleagues for advice as to whether there was any definitive therapy available. I hasten to add that you do not need to be a physician to make a list of options. A physician friend can help you frame the options, but you can also research the disease online, seek a second opinion, or both.

Some emergencies may necessitate an immediate response. These might include a car accident, a heart attack, a stroke, or an overwhelming infection. Other diagnoses, such as cancer, present a complex number of choices. I used to teach my medical students that once you mention the word cancer, the patient and spouse usually cannot hear anything else they are told. Keeping that in mind, someone might need to help the couple prepare the list of options for therapy before seeking medical help. *Always gather the best information before determining a course of action.*

Determining the Course of Action

The doctors we consulted recommended that we see whether her cognition improved with steroids. If so, then palliative[1] brain radiation would be appropriate. All of the doctors recommended only palliative care unless the steroid test was positive. Then low-level total brain radiation was administered to decrease the dose of steroids, which in itself has significant complications. This steroid test did, in fact, improve Leanne's cognition significantly.

Armed with that information, we sought an oncologist who could counsel us on the most beneficial course. We already knew that immunotherapy would not succeed due to the blood brain barrier and the inability of immunoglobulins to pass into the central nervous system. The oncologist told us that chemotherapy with small molecules also was not an option in view of many visible and hypothetically unseen metastases. He recommended a course of total brain radiation accompanied by palliative care.

---

[1] Relieving or soothing the symptoms of a disease or disorder without effecting a cure.

Once again, Jonathan came with us to the oncologist's office to be sure that we heard everything correctly. *It is important to have a person accompany the couple, as they might not be able to process the treatment choices properly due to their emotional fragility.*

We were able to ask questions and get forthright answers, but the four-to-six month prognosis was most depressing. Unlike those who are able to have chemotherapy or radiation therapy with a potential for a cure, there was no denying that a cure was not possible. Beyond praying for divine intervention, there was no other option than to make Leanne's passage from earth to eternity as comfortable as possible.

Under these unbearable circumstances, I noted that Leanne was able to cope better than I. Of course, there were times when we held each other and cried. On other occasions, Leanne told me that she was afraid but, on balance, I observed an equanimity that I had not seen before in the face of unexpected death. *Leanne lived her life verse by faith.*

> Be anxious for nothing, but in everything by prayer and supplication with thanksgiving let your requests be made known to God, and the peace of God, which surpasses all understanding, will guard your hearts and minds through Christ Jesus. —Phil. 4:6-7

Implementing the Course of Action

I asked Leanne whether she would like to stay at home throughout the course of her illness. She stated emphatically yes. Jonathan kindly volunteered to be the "chief operating officer." He reasoned, correctly, that it would be very difficult for me to manage all of the decisions unless someone presented the options and then allowed me to decide which ones to implement.

For example, we lived in a home that had many steps from one level to another and others out into the yard. Jonathan worked up options for the remodeling of our home so that there would be ramps inside and outside our home making it wheelchair friendly. He presented options to me and, once I made the decisions, he and Frank implemented them with a builder.

Jon and Frank also arranged for the installation of chairlifts up the stairs. A subsequent decision was whether to install the chairlifts permanently which we did so that I could eventually use them and remain in our home as long as possible. All of the decisions relating to the alteration of our home were resolved through discussions led by Jonathan with his siblings.

Leanne had always enjoyed gardening. Our children, under Frank's leadership, planned to landscape the yard to make it as beautiful as possible in the early spring. The azaleas were in full bloom in April. The boys set out to enable Leanne to enjoy as many days out on the patio as possible. Of course, there were moments of "vigorous discussion" when Leanne wanted something done differently. On those occasions, we scurried around to make it happen her way!

Fortunately, our daughter Debbie did not work outside the home. Her husband, Richard, and their seven children were able to manage the household responsibilities so that Debbie could spend almost half of Leanne's illness with us on multiple visits from her home in Tennessee. Our daughter Peggy worked in an office and used her vacation time to be with her mother. Between them, they were able to coordinate their schedules seamlessly so that one of them was with Leanne.

Both Debbie and Peggy are nurses and their skills were invaluable in providing care for Leanne and in gently supervising the aides. They also took turns being with us during the radiation therapy. Our daughter-in-law, Nellie, was a constant encourager. She brought their young girls over to visit Grammy frequently. Of course, each family member brings his or her gifts and resources to aid the person with a life-threatening illness. Remember that the magnitude of the gift is not as important as the magnitude of love. *Love is the most important ingredient for life, especially during the process of dying.*

Planning for Life after Death

We often think about life after death for the person who is dying, but it was also important for me to think about my own life after Leanne's death. In both my medical and ministry experience, I learned that it is extremely important for couples to discuss what the surviving spouse should do to implement their unfinished goals. In cases of sudden death, that is not possible. For example, my mother lamented for years that she could not say goodbye to my father when he died suddenly of his only heart attack at the age of forty-five, In counseling couples, I urge them to discuss forthrightly what their plans should be after the death of one of the spouses. "Be prepared" is more than a Boy Scout motto!

It was very important for me to understand Leanne's desires during her illness, but just as importantly, how she wished me to live after her death. I broached the topic with care. We had already given each other the permission to remarry, but we each stated that we did not want to do so. Therefore, we were able to discuss how I should use the remainder of my time on earth with the certainty that I would not remarry.

She urged that I start a fellowship ministry for widowers. She went further by asking the builder, Carey Hoobler, who was constructing the ramps in and around the house, to extend the patio to provide a cooking area separate from the seating area. This way we could use the two patios for outdoor entertaining. She also wanted me to continue the ministry that we frequently had with young married couples. Her vision was to use our home for fellowship lunches after church. She also requested that I support the senior pastor.

Finally, I asked her what I should do about work. At seventy-seven, I had begun to decrease my workload so that we could spend more time together as "empty-nesters" when our daughter Lorrie moved to her sister's home. In response to my query, Leanne pumped her fist into the air and exclaimed in a loud voice, "Go for it, full time." We also discussed what I should do to support the family and how I should manage our finances. Later, we had to do one of the most difficult things together: revise our wills. Because of my chronic heart disease, I had always assumed that I would die first. It was inconceivable to me that I would survive Leanne's passing. Thus, with great emotion and tenderness, we completed the most difficult and heart-wrenching planning for what would become my *suddenly single* life.

Our Walk in the Final Months

During the one hundred and four days between Leanne's diagnosis and passing, we had a number of important decisions that we had to make together. Because the family wanted Leanne's final days to be as enjoyable as possible, we needed to respect and follow her wishes, not ours. The radiation therapy schedule made some of these decisions for us, such as travel, by keeping us close to home until it was completed.

Another important decision was to ascertain what Leanne wanted to do about visits by family and friends. She decided that she wanted an open door so that as many people as possible could visit. If it were my decision, I might have decided to limit visitors, but it was important to respect her wishes. Debbie coordinated the visitations so that she did not get too tired, but it seemed as if every day people were visiting Leanne in our home. She had ministered to very many women during our twenty-four years in Washington, so she had a busy schedule, but she thrived on it!

Friends often commented that Leanne comforted them more than they comforted Leanne. Although she never enunciated it, I think Leanne was trying to prepare us and make it easy for us as she passed from this world to the next. Our pastor summed up her journey as, "One you did not wish to take, but it was with the companion of your choice, Jesus."

Four major activities occupied most of our time. First, all of our children and their families came to visit on more than one occasion. This gave Leanne an opportunity to speak to each of the grandchildren and share her wisdom with them, thereby providing important memories. In fact, one of our granddaughters wrote an essay about her grandma for a school project. My brother and his wife and Leanne's sister and her husband visited as well.

Second, Jonathan recommended that we have professional pictures taken of Leanne with as many of our children's families as possible. We also took many pictures of friends when they came to visit. This was an extraordinary gift because it provided us with photographic memories that we dearly treasure.

Third, Leanne enjoyed getting out of the house for lunch in the village. She walked at first, and then she used the three-wheel walker and, finally, the wheelchair.

Fourth, Leanne had hosted an intergenerational Bible study in our home for seventeen years. It began with a request by Dianne, who was in our Young Married's Sunday school class. Her mother did not live nearby and she was looking for mentoring from older women. There were five younger women and five older women who studied and shared life stories together. When Leanne got sick, they visited her once or twice a week, singing and sharing. It was particularly meaningful to Leanne to continue this activity. She wanted her life to be as normal as possible during these arduous days. *I observed her faith grow as her body weakened!*

Photo 6: Leanne's Intergenerational Bible Study

One very emotionally laden decision involved selecting our burial place. Leanne and I had postponed this decision as many couples do. Leanne favored burial in the ground and I favored cremation. I also thought it would be better to be in a military cemetery. Leanne leaned toward a private cemetery. How could we reach an agreement? Jonathan came to the rescue.

We took some pictures of Alexandria National Cemetery, the first national cemetery established during the Civil War era. It is a small, five-and-one-half-acre cemetery near Old Town Alexandria in Virginia. It became the first integrated national cemetery when the Buffalo Soldiers were buried there. Civilians, the four people who caught John Wilkes Booth, are also buried there.

Armed with the pictures, Jonathan asked Leanne where she would like to be buried. She favored the Alexandria National Cemetery. Touchingly, she concluded that since my life had been one of service, a military cemetery was the right spot. Furthermore, because most of the graves dated between 1862 and 1865, it was a quiet pastoral location unlike Arlington National Cemetery. It was not a gathering place for tourists and it was only twenty-eight miles from our home. With the decision made, I set out alone and disconsolate for the Quantico Marine base to secure a resting place for my wife's remains. Lorrie and I will also be there on a hilly spot near a large oak tree. Although this was a beautiful setting, I could only contemplate gloom.

During her illness, Leanne was very thoughtful in making memories for our children, grandchildren, and me. As different families visited, Leanne took time for one-on-one conversations with each person. It was a blessing that Frank and Jonathan lived nearby, Peggy and Debbie spent significant time in our home during Leanne's illness, and Lorrie lived with us. This gave Leanne a lot of time to visit with each child. She also asked me to transcribe a letter to the children when she could no longer write and complex thoughts were difficult for her to express.

May 29, 2008

To my precious children:

I decided to write to all of you together so you will know the deep love that I have for each of you. I have had so many precious moments during this time of sitting and reflecting on the myriad of memories throughout the years. Your father has been my complete and deepest love. My second fulfilling joy and completeness of my life has been being your mom. It has been wonderful to watch each of you grow and mature in your own special way. Thank you for all you have done for me throughout the years.

Loving you now and through eternity,

Mom

And the peace of God, that passes all understanding, will guard your minds and hearts in Christ Jesus. –Philippians 4:7

On Father's Day, Leanne gave me a remarkable present. After our Father's Day dinner, she sent me upstairs and asked the children to help her to the chair next to my chair at the dining room table. In fact, one of the children was apprehensive that she was going to give them a lecture. Then she called me downstairs and I was surprised to see her sitting with a big grin near my seat at the table.

Peggy took the present out of the bag and Leanne gave it to me with love sparkling in her eyes. She selected a Lladro porcelain statue of a young couple on the beach. It reminded her of our time spent in La Jolla. As I looked at the beautiful porcelain, I cried. It is my most treasured gift from our fifty-one years together. It resides on a special place on our mantelpiece along with a number of other mementos including the dried flowers from her floral arrangement.

Leanne also presented me with a lovely Father's Day card that she picked out herself. Again, since she could no longer write, Peggy transcribed her thoughts. This is Leanne's final written message to me: "You have been and always will be the light of my life. I love you more than life itself." She asked Peggy to sign it, "Your loving wife forever and ever, Leanne."

Photo 7: Lladro Porcelain Statue - Father's Day Gift

Day by day, we could see changes in Leanne. Her hair fell out as she showered. She decided to not wear a wig. With her usual sense of humor, she looked in the mirror one day and said, "I think I look like a plucked chicken!" Then as the tumors continued to grow, she developed weakness in her arms first and then her legs. It was difficult for her to stand; nevertheless, she pulled herself up to hug each visitor for as long as standing was possible.

The growth of the tumors further compromised Leanne's cognition in a way similar to rapidly progressing Alzheimer's disease. The tumors relentlessly interrupted neuronal function and nerve conduction in her brain. We adapted to this by using shorter sentences in conversation so that she could understand us better. I must admit, it was terrible to observe her rapid decline. Yet, Leanne was content. She repeatedly asked with ever-increasing frequency, "Is it wrong to have so much joy?" It was as if her life's Bible verse was being fulfilled before my eyes.

Fortunately, Leanne could recognize and talk to all of us throughout her illness. We slept together as long as we could in our bedroom on the second floor. We also enjoyed being able to hold each other as we fell asleep. We savored every moment of tenderness we were granted. One night, Debbie brought us a lovely dinner that we ate by candlelight in our bedroom.

Difficult Physical Challenges

We set up a chair for Leanne in the shower and arranged for the use of the chairlift and a potty chair so that she would not have to walk to the bathroom. But eventually, Peggy and I faced the difficult task of finding a service that provided qualified aides. Someone needed to be with Leanne during the day to help with light housework, transport her to and from the car, bathe, and dress her. On the lighter side, I had great difficulty putting her bra on her correctly. While I did dress her at times, it was clearly more comfortable for Leanne if an aide or one of our daughters showered her. The aides became an integral part of our "caring circle." Debbie's two daughters, Sarah and Abigail, even stayed with us for three weeks to help Jonathan and Nellie manage their children and to give us extra help as Leanne became weaker.

Transporting Leanne from the bed to the nearby commode was scary at times. It was hard for her to maintain her balance and she needed assistance to make a ninety-degree turn to settle on the seat. We laughed about the irony of a physician taking care of the bodily functions of a nurse. It is usually the other way around.

Our evening ritual began with Leanne taking the chair lift to the landing at the top of the steps. At the landing there was a ninety-degree turn and two more steps to reach the second floor. The hospice nurse advised me to let Leanne go if she began to fall while navigating the steps. I vowed never to acquiesce to that admonition. As time progressed, it was impossible for Leanne to navigate those two steps without having someone behind her and me in front of her holding her hands.

Tori Voth from the women's Bible study lived close by and kindly agreed to come over every night to help Leanne up the two steps from the landing to the second floor. From there she got Leanne into the transport chair and into bed. As I observed these evening rituals, and how Tori, our daughters, and other women cared for Leanne, I realized that women have a special need for female friends. *The nurturing spirit of the women who helped us was of great comfort in these times of duress.*

Climbing the two stairs became progressively more difficult for Leanne, so Debbie recommended that we put a hospital bed in the living room. She made it look beautiful and welcoming with a pink bedspread, a pink pillowcase, and flowers. Then we pondered how we could suggest to Leanne the idea of staying in the hospital bed permanently. Debbie came up with a great solution. One day, she calmly asked Leanne if she would like to lie down on the hospital bed for her nap rather than going upstairs to sleep in our bed. Leanne thought that was a good idea. With tears in my eyes, I watched my dear wife acquiesce to a change from sleeping with me upstairs to spending the rest of her days in the hospital bed. Leanne had no sooner settled in the bed than Lorrie came home from work and said in a loud voice, "Mother, what are you doing in that bed?" We calmly replied that she was taking a nap. This answer satisfied Lorrie, but grieved us deeply.

Initially, I was able to sleep on a cot next to Leanne's bed. We would fall asleep holding hands after the last aide left at midnight. There were humorous moments, too. One evening, our son Jonathan, who weighs about 140 pounds and is shorter than I, was able to crawl into the hospital bed next to his mom while the rail was up. Leanne enjoyed having Jonathan beside her in the bed, so, on another day, she asked me—at five-foot-eight inches and a hundred-eighty-five pounds—to do the same. While I was able to crawl into the bed with the rail up, my arm and leg eventually became numb. When I was ready to get up, I could not get the rail down and extract myself from the bed without help!

Since no one was home to help me, I decided to slide down and over the rail as carefully as I could. Unfortunately, there was a flower vase above my head. As I moved, I hit the bedside table and down came the vase right on my jaw. Thankfully, it was low enough that I did not lose any teeth. Leanne awoke and I managed to extricate myself. If the vase had hit two inches higher, I would have lost my front teeth. We laughed about it and decided I would never crawl inside the bed again.

As Leanne became much weaker, it took two of us to change her position. We used the nursing trick of pulling the sheet with the person on it and rolling it from side to side. We also moved from two shifts of aides to three. In this phase of palliative care, pain management and bowel function were the most important concerns. Catheterization of her bladder was required occasionally to manage urination. One or both of our daughters assisted me throughout this most difficult time. We also set up room dividers in order to maintain as much of Leanne's dignity as possible.

As the summer wore on, I began to think Leanne was holding on to celebrate Jonathan's August 2 birthday. We tried to make the celebration joyful. Nellie and Jonathan's three girls, ages five, three, and one, accompanied them to Leanne's bedside. We all sang happy birthday to Jonathan. Leanne was so happy to be able to have some cake and join in the celebration, particularly with the grandchildren present.

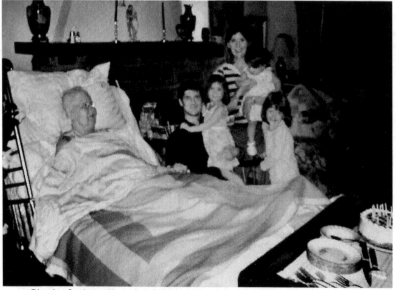

Photo 8: Jonathan's birthday party with Nellie and their Girls

On Aug. 3, 2008 we noted a significant change in Leanne's condition. The hospice physician we consulted thought Leanne had about two more weeks to live. Debbie intuitively came to Washington that day. Peggy was already here helping me. We decided that Lorrie should continue to work because we were not sure how she could handle seeing the passing of her mother. That evening Leanne was quite talkative and responsive, but by midnight she began to have respiratory distress.

We kept ahead of the pain using oral morphine. During the night, her respirations were labored and she began experiencing rapid gasping and accelerated breathing. We were deeply worried about how much longer she could survive. In the morning, Peggy dressed her in a beautiful clean nightgown. I had planned to have a communion service for our four children and Leanne so everyone with the exception of Lorrie, who went to work, was gathered in our home at 8:30 a.m.

By the time our children arrived, Leanne's respirations were extremely rapid and labored. I held her closely and whispered to her repeatedly that it was all right to go to be with our Lord. We called the hospice nurse at around 10:00 a.m. When she came to Leanne's bedside, I stepped back from holding Leanne while the nurse came over and whispered, "It is all right to go now." I went back to Leanne's side and held her tightly telling her repeatedly how much I loved her. Within a few minutes, my dear Leanne gasped her last breath. *I cried uncontrollably!*

Lessons Learned

1. The onset of a fatal illness brings a cacophony of emotional turmoil. There are heavy overtones of regret, guilt, anger, disappointment, fear, and depression. It is extremely important to navigate these emotionally cascading waters as skillfully as possible to provide a harmonious nest of comfort for the person who is passing from this world to the next.

2. There frequently are unfinished agendas and discussions. If possible, make plans ahead of time for living arrangements of the surviving spouse. Ascertain what your spouse would like you to complete on behalf of both of you. Reconciliation with members of family or friends is imperative at this time of life.

3. Many decisions must be made in a timely fashion. One must choose the proper therapies, where to spend the final days, and decide how many visitors to allow at one time. It was essential to maintain Leanne's control over her life as long as possible. It is particularly important to develop a "circle of care" composed of family members and friends to assist both partners during this journey. We also had to determine how to make our home suitable for Leanne to remain at home as long as possible and to take little trips that she enjoyed. The final resting place for both of us needed to be determined. So many decisions needed to be made in the space of a few heart-wrenching days.

4. It is important to ascertain the final wishes of the departing spouse relative to how the surviving spouse should live and carry out the couple's legacy. Some examples of what Leanne and I decided follow.

   a) Leanne asked me to start a monthly home fellowship that would include a Sunday meal for widowers.
   b) She encouraged me to offer our home for social functions to the Young Married Class.
   c) We made plans on how I should contribute to the education of the grandchildren and great grandchildren. Also to be of financial support to our children as appropriate.
   d) Leanne asked me to support our pastor.

e) She told me to stop reducing my work schedule and to return to work full time.

f) She suggested ways for me to assume some of the many household responsibilities she performed.

5. If a spouse decides to remain at home during the dying process, the home will need to be altered to enable mobility. Care must be taken to ensure bathroom safety and to have facilities to manage bodily functions with modesty. This will frequently involve assistance of the surviving spouse in ways never contemplated. Yet, this very opportunity of intimate sharing can lead to the most profound depth of love. The process of dying is a normal part of living. It is not to be feared, whitewashed, or repressed. Nevertheless, the death of a spouse is a great tragedy for the surviving person. A kaleidoscope of conflicting emotions and thoughts attends it. One's life is irrevocably altered! As one becomes *suddenly single,* be prepared for enormous emotional upheavals. It frequently evokes a feeling of helplessness and great tragedy even though each of us must face it. Be sure to have someone who can help manage the daily situations, act as a sounding board, and provide balance in this very threatening and fragile time.

6. The death of a spouse brings down the curtain on relationships that existed for many years within the family. For the husband who loses his cherished wife, there is frequently a feeling of overwhelming grief, anger, depression, guilt, confusion, and loss of the will to live. Men tend to retreat into themselves at these times. Avoid this natural tendency! Family, particularly, younger children and grandchildren, can provide the impetus for living. Men find it is often awkward to be in previously comfortable situations and social settings. You may find it is especially difficult to be around married friends. I did! Such encounters heighten the sense of loss and underscore the feeling of being alone. However, be very careful to avoid new relationships until sufficient time for adjustment has occurred. Also, be aware that grief can come on suddenly, producing loneliness even in a crowd.

7. Even if one's faith has been the center of life, the irreversible separation precipitated by death is a shattering experience of cataclysmic proportions. *One will wonder — why, God why?*

8. Remarriage is a most important topic for discussion and should be explored before the crisis. A person's view of faith, marriage, intimacy, and communication while one's spouse is alive will shape one's views about the future. It was not until the second wedding anniversary after Leanne passed that I realized that the phrase in our wedding vows, "till death do we part," is an option, not a command (see page 82).

3

Overcome with Grief

On the rebound one passes into tears and pathos. Maudlin tears. I almost prefer the moments of agony. These are at least clean and honest. But the path of self-pity, the wallow, the loathsome, sticky-sweet pleasure of indulging it—that disgusts me. —C. S. Lewis

The onset of grief will depend on the circumstances surrounding the death of a spouse. If death is sudden and unexpected, the spouse will grieve the loss of not being able to say goodbye. Grief will begin before death if there is a warning that death is coming, such as, with the diagnosis of a life-threatening illness. But no amount of preparation can equip one for the total catastrophic shock that occurs when your spouse dies. Even though I prayed that God would spare Leanne from more suffering, when she died after a few hours of labored, gasping respirations, the finality of her death was overwhelming. For many days, the shroud of grief appeared and disappeared like a cloak on a dark dismal night.

The Immediate Aftermath of Death

In spite of having helped many families in the immediate aftermath of a loved one's death, I was unprepared for the wrenching separation this final moment brought. I held Leanne for a while after she passed and gave her a final kiss goodbye. Then the children had individual private time with their mother to say their goodbyes. Debbie, Peggy, and I went to the NIH cafeteria where Lorrie was working. When she came out of the locker room, we told her that her mother had died. We all went home together and Lorrie said goodbye to her mother.

After about an hour, I called the funeral home and they came to transport Leanne's body to the funeral parlor. It is important to know that the undertaker usually strips the person's body of all clothes in the absence of the family and then places the person in a body bag. I insisted that they carefully lift Leanne into the body bag by the sheets and not close the bag while inside our home. As was the case with most husbands of my era, I had carried Leanne across the threshold of each new home. I felt it was essential that

I be with Leanne when she left our home for the last time. I wanted her to leave dressed in her nightgown in dignity with the body bag open.

The immediate aftermath of the passing of a spouse is a turbulent sea of crashing emotions. I revisited the guilt of not making the diagnosis of her cancer sooner. I pondered the various things that I could have done differently throughout our marriage. I administered self-flagellation. At other times, I enjoyed pleasant memories. I cried at the slightest provocation such as looking at a picture, seeing an empty chair, or remembering a phrase that she uttered. I learned I could be alone and despondent in the midst of a family gathering where each of us was searching for ways to cope with the passing of such a dynamic person in our lives.

Photo 9: Back Row L-R, Nellie, Julia, Debbie
Front Row L-R, Jonathan, Katie, Frank, Bella, Leanne, Jonathan Rapp

Just before her body entered the hearse, I zipped up the body bag and stared down at its black exterior overcome with great cascading sorrow. My sorrow was darker than the blackness of the bag. I somehow muttered goodbye to the undertaker and returned to our home. *A large part of my life departed with her!*

I felt that I needed to make the numerous arrangements at the funeral home alone. I picked out a coffin used in cremation, an urn, and the picture for Leanne's prayer card. I made the myriad of other arrangements that are necessary when a person passes. After making these decisions, I invited our children to come to the funeral parlor to finalize arrangements.

I could not cope with the countless details. While I have done all of these things for members of the congregation, it was entirely different when it was necessary to make final arrangements for my wife. Even now, I can clearly recall only a few details of that week. All of our children were with me and they lightened the burden of making so many decisions. For instance, Jonathan helped with the obituary, since that was too difficult for me. He was also the one who made all of the contacts with the media. Debbie organized the cards and letters. While I deeply appreciated all of the expressions of sympathy, reading them only accentuated my sorrow.

We then made arrangements to use the church for the memorial service and the reception. I discussed the format of the memorial service with our senior pastor. I agonized over whether or not I should be the one to conduct it. Fortunately, he gently convinced me that my role was to be the chief mourner.

Finally, I wrote the poem for Leanne's prayer card, which was a difficult, but loving task. I tearfully wrote the following poem as I meditated on our bonded life.

In Loving memory of Leanne Young

God spoke His Word with Creative love
And Leanne responded to the call from above.
You reflected this love in so many ways.
It guided your path throughout your days.

Your mission in life was nurturing care,
To those in need almost anywhere,
Especially your family both near and far,
Accompanying your husband—his burdens to share.

Your road was at times a difficult path,
As God chose you to care for a special lass,
For fifty years you mothered and guided her,
Until now, she will fly to another.[2]

---

[2] This is a reference to our daughter, Lorrie, whose learning disability resulted in her living with us for fifty years prior to moving in with her sister's family.

You cared for family as health ebbed and flowed.
You mentored with wisdom in your twinkling glow,
Until your own body began to fail,
And you gracefully trod on without a wail.

On April 23—that terrible day
Metastatic brain cancer began to take you away,
As we accompanied you for a very short time,
You gracefully showed us that "Jesus is mine!"

Photo 10: Leanne Young

On one of many trips to the funeral home, I went down the wrong hall and stumbled upon the spot where Leanne's body was on a gurney outside the refrigerated storage space. Leanne was beautifully dressed and prepared for visitation. After I recovered from the shock, I asked if they could take her body to a room where I could stay with her for a while. It was a great comfort to have a quiet time to compose my thoughts and "talk" to her before the visitation hours. It was our last time to be "alone together." *I began to realize that staying behind and helping one's spouse move from this world to the next was part of love's final gifts.*

One week after Leanne's death, the memorial service was held in our church. It was like a dream. I was numb and sobbing intermittently. I just could not comprehend that it was happening.

The tributes of our children and friends gave me momentary solace and our pastor's words, now forgotten, were of transient, but significant comfort. As I listened later to a recording of the memorial service, I appreciated the beautiful outpouring of love.

The reception was a similar blur. I greeted the people on emotional autopilot. It was as if I was watching another person. I appreciated the presence of so many well-wishers, but I have only a few memories of those who attended. No words can adequately explain the extent of the emotional collapse I experienced.

When we returned home, the family gathered. Although I did not wish to eat, our family insisted. Each of the children's families circled, absorbed in their own grief. For the first time, I realized what was to become a frequent emotion, to feel alone in the midst of a crowd. Now there was nothing to do other than await the final act of committing Leanne's ashes to the ground.

The next morning, our family, our pastor, and a few friends completed the sorrowful task of placing Leanne's urn into the ground and saying a final goodbye. Covering that beautiful green urn, the same kind that would contain Lorrie's and my ashes someday, was a dreadful and painful experience. As I glanced around at the white military headstones in neat rows, I had a flashback memory of a military review where those buried were at parade rest.

The next day, our daughter Lorrie left for Tennessee with her sister's family where she would reside in her newly constructed apartment. In the short space of a few months, our nuclear family was reduced to our dog and me. Now I needed to prepare to live alone, *suddenly single*. I was a widower. I despised that label!

The First Week

As previously mentioned, the week between the death and burial of a loved one is a swirl of great activity, packed with trivial and heartbreaking details. For example, Peggy and Frank helped me determine which of Leanne's clothes I would keep. They also helped arrange the kitchen to suit my limited experience in preparing food. I also had to design a prayer card, organize the memorial service, plan a reception for family and friends, and meet an endless stream of well-wishers. All of this activity carried me down a turbulent river of white-water rapids battering me with both memories and regrets.

I was distraught! My appetite was gone, my bed was now empty, and I longed for Leanne's presence. Yet, there was so much to do in a frenetic home packed with family and friends. It was a nightmarish dream world and a time of intense confusion. The dominant themes of this tragic week were guilt, longing, and relief.

Like many men in my situation, I had survivor's guilt. I was also guilty of not identifying the diagnosis myself. I also felt a deep longing for Leanne's companionship. We had always shared our thoughts and feelings whenever we faced crises. Now, to do so alone was heartbreaking. At the same time, I felt relief that her suffering was finally over.

A *suddenly single* spouse experiences a crescendo of discordant feelings. It is like listening to music performed by musicians who are playing notes off of different pages. The state of mind will vary depending on the length and depth of the marriage relationship, faith, and the cause of death.

I am grateful that I had an opportunity to say goodbye to my dear wife. When sudden death denies the surviving spouse of a chance to say goodbye, there may be a profound sense of loss of closure. Unfinished and unresolved issues can tear at the fabric of the family left behind. A turbulent marriage can result in a haunting grief from the lack of reconciliation. Becoming *suddenly single* also evokes questions about mortality. The song "Flowers Never Bend with the Rainfall" by Simon and Garfunkel describes one of the mechanisms for coping with death.

> The mirror on my wall
> Casts an image dark and small
> But I'm not sure at all it's my reflection.
>
> I am blinded by the light
> Of God and truth and right
> And I wander in the night without direction.
>
> So I'll continue to continue to pretend
> My life will never end,
> And flowers never bend
> With the rainfall.

Even C. S. Lewis, when confronted by the death of his wife, questioned why God was not a greater comfort during this time of profound duress.[3] In my case, I was more confused by the purpose of my unexpected additional years. I even thought of stopping my cardiovascular medications and running up and down the stairs to precipitate a sudden death due to cardiac arrhythmia. I pushed away this fleeting thought of self-murder as a violation of the Ten Commandments.[4] Such selfishness would only compound the anguish of our children.

Let me share a brief word on death by suicide. Suicide often leaves surviving loved ones in profound mental torment frequently amalgamated by guilt, and anger. In a tortured, sensitive, and emotion-laden letter to her husband who committed suicide, a woman described her emotions. Her thoughts are included in the footnote.[5] They illustrate the feelings of many who confront a loved one's death by suicide.

Depression and sleeplessness are frequent companions of bereavement. While Leanne was declining, I found that Xanax was essential for dispelling my dark mood. Immediately after her death, I found it extraordinarily difficult to fall asleep. I usually stayed up until I was no longer able to remain alert and then slept fitfully for only about five hours. Getting up was a chore.

---

[3] "Meanwhile, where is God …? When you are happy, so happy that you have no sense of needing Him, so happy that you are tempted to feel His claims on you as an interruption, if you remember yourself and turn to Him in gratitude and praise, you will be—or so it feels—welcomed with open arms. But go to Him when your need is desperate, when all other help is vain, and what do you find? A door slammed closed in your face and a sound of bolting and double bolting on the inside. You may as well turn away. The longer you wait, the more emphatic the silence will become." C. S. Lewis, *A Grief Observed*. Harper San Francisco, 1961, pg. 17-18.

[4] Dennis P. Hollinger, "A Theology of Death." In *Suicide: A Christian Response* [ed.] Timothy J. Demy and Gary P. Stewart, Kregel Publications, 1998, pg. 257-267.

[5] "Dear Mark, how could someone I know so well deceive me? Your note said 'I'm sorry, I'm not well, I'm no good.' This is what you left for a legacy for your loving wife of 33 years and three beautiful children who respected, adored and loved you, a big brother who called you his best friend, and so many others I couldn't begin to count, who were impressed by your work ethic, sense of humor, sincerity, and respected you as a solid Christian man. All the good you did in your life is now *shadowed* by the way you ended your life." Gary P. Stewart "Suicide's Companion: A Trail of Tears." In *Suicide: A Christian Response* [ed.] Timothy J. Demy and Gary P. Stewart, Kregel Publications, 1998, pg. 430.

Elizabeth Kûbler-Ross describes five generally accepted stages encountered in dying: denial and isolation, anger, bargaining, depression, and acceptance.[6] Our fear of death is largely a product of our understanding and beliefs about life. We often view death as an enemy that is repressed, something that happens to others. Yet death was not always isolated from the cycle of life.

Pastor John Fanestil has noted that some members of his congregation died "peaceful [sic] and experienced good deaths." In exploring this phenomenon, he found an interesting article in the July-August 1801 issue of *Armenian Magazine* that was entitled "An account of Mrs. Hunter's Holy Life and Happy Death."[7] The author, John Wood, cited many excerpts in which the faith of this twenty-six-year-old woman, Mrs. Hunter, changed her view of death from despair to praise. This concept of a "happy death" was common in the nineteenth century.

The death of a spouse forces the partner to re-examine and challenge bedrock beliefs. Vital questions suddenly and forcibly confront us. What happens after death? What is the meaning of life? What is the meaning of death? What happens to me after I die? As C. S. Lewis wandered along his path of grief, he recorded his questioning of long-held beliefs.[8]

My journey to the other side of grief, described in the next chapter, is a continual process of answering new questions about the meaning of life. It began as Leanne was in the process of passing from this world to the next. On the day of her death, I wrote a simple note, part of which is included in the footnotes.[9] This will provide a glimpse of my first month of wandering on this new pathway of grief. While this grief persisted for more than two years, its complexion changed dramatically. Now, I experience a

---

[6] Elizabeth Kûbler-Ross, *On Death and Dying*, McMillan, 1970.

[7] John Fanestil, *Mrs. Happy Death*, Doubleday, New York, 2006, pg. 4.

[8] "I wrote last night. It was a yell rather than a thought. Let me try it over again. Is it rational to believe in a bad God? Anyway, in a God so bad as all that? The Cosmic Sadist, the spiteful imbecile." C. S. Lewis, ibid., pg. 43.

[9] "I do not know if you heard me talk to you as you were dying but I told you repeatedly that I loved you and thanked you for all that you have done for our family and me. After you left, I cried uncontrollably. I then read your Scripture, talked with you and prayed with you. Each of the children said their goodbyes as well. It was the most difficult day in my life. After you pass from this world to the next, we went over and got Lorrie so that she could say her goodbyes."

continual feeling of her presence within my mind and being. As I told our family, "As long as one of us is here, both of us are here." Yet, I confess that grief still suddenly washes over me.

The Acute Phase: First Month

Because of this incredible fracture of our bonded life, I decided to avoid contact with others as much as possible for thirty days. My intention was to review our marriage, synthesize a new single life, and determine how to integrate our agreed-upon goals into an action plan. During this time, I did little other than contemplate how to live! Amid great sorrow and tears, I tried to understand the events leading to Leanne's departure. My dominant emotion was a deep dark sense of emptiness coupled with a loss of interest in life. Counterbalancing these foreboding and nihilistic thoughts were expressions of concern from the children such as, "Take care of yourself, we cannot lose you, too."

It was extraordinarily difficult to go to bed at night, wake up in the morning, and prepare food. I attempted to write, but my mind was like a bowl of mush. I merely wandered around our house, talking aloud to Leanne, still in a state of shock—reliving those final days and flagellating myself for not being able to diagnose Leanne's cancer at a stage where definitive treatment rather than palliative care could have prolonged her life. I deeply regretted that we did not have more time together.

I read her life verse often, Philippians 4:6-7.[10] I was desperately searching for the joy that she experienced as she was passing from this world to the next. It confused me because my life was anything but joyful. I rarely recorded my prayers, but I did so by accident on Aug. 22, 2008. I often use a speech recognition program when I write at the computer and I had neglected to turn off the microphone. I began to pray aloud and, unbeknownst to me, I recorded my prayer of supplication. I have included it in the footnotes.[11]

---

[10] "Be anxious for nothing, but in everything by prayer and supplication, with thanksgiving, let your requests be made known to God and the peace of God, which passes all understanding, will guard your hearts and minds through Christ Jesus."

[11] "In the midst of pain, Aug. 22, 2008, Dear Lord, I am in great emotional trouble. You have blessed me over the years with grace for which I am very thankful. You have given me a wonderful wife, Leanne, to whom I have been

In retrospect, I realize that this intense period of solitary contemplation was my attempt to control the grief process. Nevertheless, it was a necessary part of coping. As the thirty days of contemplation came to an end, I wrote a letter to the children to summarize the basic building blocks that embodied our marriage and this special time in the winter of our lives.[12]

---

married for fifty-one years. During these many years, we have had the privilege of birthing five children, seeing their marriages, and the fruit of those unions. On Aug. 4, you called her home. I observed that you filled her with grace and peace and I believe she was traveling between heaven and earth in those last few days. The words that she said in the last few days 'is it wrong for me to have so much joy' shows me that she was looking forward to being with you. And I'm pleased that she is free from the emotional and physical pain of her cancer. She faced her loss of function gracefully and you held her in your hand. Nevertheless, I am in much in pain because I miss her so acutely. I thank you for the comfort of the hymn 'Abide With Me.' I do pray now, oh Lord, that you will forgive my many sins, the times that I've been arrogant, the times that I've not supported the family as I should, the times that I've not been as gracious as you would have me to be. Lord I know that I have sinned and come short of your glory just as it says in Romans 3:23. I do hope and earnestly pray Lord that you will help me through this difficult time. Please, help me show forth your grace that I might glorify you in all I do. I thank you for each one of my family who have supported both mom and me in many ways. Please, help each of them in their grief and sorrow. Comfort them and help them to be restored and to see heaven with the same clear eyes as Leanne did. Now as I turn to work, please be with me and live in my mind with your Spirit to help me to focus on you as I do my job. To you be glory and praise."

[12]"I decided that this weekend I needed to be alone to think about Mom and our married life together. It was only four months ago on this past Saturday that the diagnosis was made. We then began our journey 'for a time certain.' Throughout this entire difficult and unexpected journey, your mother displayed remarkable grace, caring, nurturing, and, yes, at times grieving. I've become more in love with my dear Babes than ever before as I saw her deal with a progressive loss of both physical and mental function. Yet, this loss was accompanied by a great growth in faith and grace. I am so glad that our children with the exception of Lorrie were present to the very end. I want to start this brief letter by thanking each one of you for the many contributions you have made to our life that gave meaning, purpose, and joy!

Mom and I have had a spectacular marriage. Two people being equally yoked together characterized our marriage. Each of us contributed to the well-being of the other. Each brought unique gifts and attributes to our marriage. My primary job was to increase the economic status of the family and to reach a very far star. Mom was the nurturer of the family, the queen of the castle, and the individual who gave

I discovered four ways to ease the pain of becoming *suddenly single* that might be of help to others in the acute phase of grief. First, on the day Leanne passed, I started a daily journal in the form of letters and poems to Leanne. Using my speech recognition software made it seem like talking to her, but with punctuation added. Thus, I could share my daily activities, thoughts, and progress in completing the goals that we decided upon during her transition. A portion of the introduction to those letters follows.

> My overwhelming grief immobilized me today and made it impossible to function. Much needed to be done between your passing and the memorial service on Aug. 11. Funeral arrangements had to be made, your prayer card poem written, floral arrangements picked out, family notified, the reception planned after the memorial service and the letters that each of the children and grandchildren wrote had to be composed. During the intense time of grief from Aug. 4 to Aug. 13, I was unable to write. Jonathan helped with the obituary and the facilitation of a news obituary. I went back and forth to the funeral home to attend to details. On one occasion, before the visitation hours on Sunday the 10th, I got lost in the funeral home and suddenly found you outside the refrigerated room. You were fully dressed and ready for visitation, but cold to my touch. At first, I was shocked but then I asked for a special time to sit with you in one of the visitation rooms. I prayed and talked to you and thanked God for the gift of you as my wife. An indescribable peace washed over me and prepared me for the difficult task of saying goodbye and the subsequent services. Visitation was on Sunday evening Aug. 10 with only the family as you requested. After our immediate family had some more time with you, I kissed you goodbye and closed the coffin lid in preparation for your cremation. On Aug. 11 we had your memorial service which was absolutely remarkable. Rob read my letter, Debbie's letter, and the three oldest grandchildren spoke. Uncle Ken made a few remarks as well. Jonathan

me the security to sally forth each day in battle. Without her great support and, at times, self-sacrifice, the family would not have succeeded. In addition, Mom had a separate ministry with women and couples. It will go on for years. She was always a much better person in one-on-one counseling than I ever could be. At our core, Mom and I have a deep and abiding faith in Jesus Christ as our Lord and Savior that has guided us throughout the years."

beautifully played his trumpet for you. Nellie and her flute teacher played a duet. After that, we had a reception in the upper room. In fact, it was the first time that the upper room was used and Rob made special provision to be sure that you had a reception there. Visitors included many people from the neighborhood, our church, and Essex Woodlands. Anne DeMaret and Jeff Himawan flew in to represent Essex Woodlands. The internment service was the next morning at Alexandria National Cemetery. I was in shock and experienced profound grief. I don't remember much of the details in these intervening days from your passing to your burial. Each of our children and grandchildren struggled with their grief and overwhelming sadness in a different way. After your internment, Lorrie traveled with Debbie and Richard to her new apartment in their addition to their home. They graciously welcomed Lorrie into their family.

Second, I resumed our devotions. I found that I could not look at the empty place where Leanne usually sat as we communed with God, so my study became the place where I had my quiet time with God. Our devotions included Bible study, sentence prayers, and hymns. This was difficult at first, but it brought a new and deeper relationship with Jesus that would transform my life.

Third, I decided to wear a black band on my forearm. It gives me a feeling of pressure and a connection with Leanne. Earlier, I wore a black band underneath my shirt in honor of my father for a year. This custom was most comforting to me as it gave me a sense of my continued marriage.

Finally, after much thought, I took off my wedding band and put it with Leanne's ring to be passed to one of the grandchildren. Both rings were engraved with our initials and the abbreviation L.T.E. (Love Through Eternity) to symbolize our commitment to each other through God's grace. I replaced it with a new wedding band inscribed, "Til We Meet Again."

Additionally, I prepared the mantelpiece as a special place in our home for the beautiful Lladro porcelain statue of a man and a woman on the seaside that Leanne picked out for me for Father's Day, 2008, as well as some other items of sentimental value. After those thirty days, I emerged with the goal to synthesize a new life. Little did I realize I was on a path to idolatry.

Lessons Learned

1. Grief begins with the diagnosis of a life-threatening disease. The process of grieving prior to death is, in part, defined by the nature of the disease, the ages of the spouses, the duration of the illness, the quality of the marriage bond, and the couple's Worldview. Family relationships are extremely important. It is imperative to reconcile conflicts before your spouse dies. Death closes a chapter in life like the slamming of an iron door!

2. While Leanne and I had sufficient time to discuss how I should carry on without her, death can come suddenly and then it is too late to make these kinds of decisions. Ideally, as part of an annual review of their marriage, a couple would discuss their legacy and how each one should live if the other dies first.

3. The loss of a wife introduces unique challenges for men. Many men, particularly, if they have been married for a long time, are not used to caring for themselves in regard to meals, domestic duties, and planning family events.

4. The sudden collapse of all of the activity surrounding the memorial service, the reception, the burial, and the departure of family members leaves one in a vulnerable, lonely state and, possibly, if not probably, even prone to depression.

5. Isolation was my escape route. I was paralyzed as the dark, dismal shroud of grief descended. Leanne's wishes, described previously, appeared as impossible missions. So, I retreated further into the solace of isolation. You will likely have similar feelings. For your own sake and that of your family, I encourage you to work through them expeditiously as possible. They need you now more than ever!

6. Meeting old friends, particularly married friends, was quite intolerable. I was the "odd man out." I despised the repeated query, "How are you doing?" In this initial phase, I avoided all outside contact except with family. The one exception was with colleagues who only knew Leanne superficially.

7. It was helpful to keep busy, particularly, with mindless tasks. It was a partial distraction from the overwhelming pain and sorrow.

8. I forced myself to follow healthy habits after an initial thought of precipitating my own demise by ceasing cardiovascular medicine and engaging in strenuous exercise. My diet was relatively easy to manage even though I did little by way of food preparation during our married life.

    I realized that a good diet, exercise, and a proper amount of sleep were very important. Sleep was elusive and even the combination of Xanax and Benadryl recommended to me by a psychiatrist did not suffice to ensure a modicum of sleep. Only sheer exhaustion induced sufficient drowsiness. It was also difficult to get up in the morning.

    If I was to go on living, I must somehow restore healthy habits.

9. My life was in a shambles as I attempted to cope with this new and painful state. I could no longer avoid the harsh reality that I was *suddenly single*! The search for the other side of grief had begun. I concluded that a great deal of work needs to be done in order to rebuild a shattered life. **Grief is hard work!**

4

The Other Side of Grief

Do not store up for yourselves treasures on earth, where moth and rust destroy and where thieves break in and steal. But store up for yourselves treasure in heaven .... For where your treasure is, there will your heart be also. —Matt. 6:19-21

G rief associated with the death of a spouse is a multistage and complex process. Previously, I described the acute phase with its attendant extreme emotional components, such as guilt, fear, depression, loneliness, sadness, regrets, anxiety, sleeplessness, loss of motivation, and foreboding. Tears and, at times, sobbing occurred with disparate provocations. The thought of a past event, the sight of an empty chair, sitting at the table alone, and visiting a familiar place we had frequented caused the greatest pain.

The Chronic Phase of Grief

There is no sharp demarcation between the acute and chronic phases. Rather, there is a slow progression as a forced adjustment occurs. In the first year after Leanne's passing, I found holidays, birthdays, and anniversaries to be extremely difficult. At times, the loneliness was overwhelming. I even felt lonely and isolated in crowds. I also exhibited classical signs of anxiety such as rapid heartbeat, loss of appetite, clumsiness, and altered sensations such as numbness and tingling in my fingers.

My discomfort and withdrawal were quite paralyzing. Visiting the cemetery became my solace even though I had always found cemeteries to be depressing. As the months dragged on, however, most of these physical and emotional signs and symptoms lessened while my visits to the cemetery continued to be the activity that provided the most comfort. *My heart was bound, in fact buried, in grief. I was not storing up treasures in heaven!*

Now alone, I was compelled to resume living without my dearest partner. A sudden fall into a dark hole replaced a deeply intimate, passionate love. Yes, I was climbing out, but the hole would remain. I wrestled, and continue to wrestle, with the reality of my great loss.

Wrestling with Reality

What is real, tangible and ultimately valuable?
Is it treasure or accomplishments or pleasure?
Does it revolve around family and friends?
Or is it something that ultimately will never end?

In life, we inhabit physical and spiritual realms.
The seen and the unseen occasionally do blend
Merging into a sphere without demarcated end.
At times, spiritual life attenuates without a sigh.

Earthbound creatures eventually die.
As loved ones leave, we grieve and cry.
We observe empty places without their faces,
Attempting to cope while wrestling in dark places.

Does reality scream they are really gone?
And if they are gone, is it to another place?
Will I see her again? Will I know her face?
The lines of certainty are difficult to trace.

Reality is not something I can see or feel.
At times, I do not know what is real.
Wrestling with Scripture—wandering without wife,
Revealed a deeper vision of salvation and eternal life.

Frank, November 15, 2010

Suddenly Single Realities

I was compelled to organize our home for single occupancy. My needs were simpler. My children helped me sort through the clothes that belonged to Leanne. I had great difficulty discarding her clothing and personal effects and kept most of her clothes in our closet and her jewelry in the drawer. I left her pink washcloth and towel exactly as it was on the towel rack in the bathroom. I knew that I was clinging to her presence. *However, that was exactly what I wanted to do.* I could not bear the suddenness of our separation.

My mother donated my father's clothes and personal effects soon after she was widowed at the age of forty-four. I found that to be quite traumatic. Her actions may have been dictated by the suddenness of our father's death after his heart attack. Life disappears so fast! I am constantly amazed at how rapidly death takes one away and, like birth, it is irreversible. Now, *suddenly single*, I felt the need to have physical vestiges of her past. I could not discard these symbols and traces of her life. In the ministry, I noted that families coped in varying ways with the harsh reality of disposing of the earthly possessions of their loved ones. *Now I realized that there is no right or wrong way of dealing with this stark reality.*

I had to begin to sort through a number of things that I avoided in the first thirty days of deep grief. Many of these were mundane tasks. For example, I had not used the washing machine or dryer for fifty-one years. Leanne had managed all of that! She prepared almost all meals. She opened and organized the mail for my review, paid the household bills, filed documents, and balanced the books for my company. Only details that required my decision were presented to me. In fact, I never managed the household money including donations to charities.

I realized for the first time how much Leanne did around the house to make my life so comfortable. I was a "well-kept man." I was embarrassed by how much I took for granted! As I pondered my new state, I wrote this poem mingled with embarrassment and regret for not being more helpful throughout the years.

Reflections on Housework While Alone

It's almost as if I lived my life in a magical home.
Leaving after breakfast and returning after work.
Confident our children were nourished with loving care.
I avoided through neglect household wear and tear.

You managed seamlessly and efficiently every day.
Possibly fairies cleaned up and cooked while I was away.
I only realized how much you did once you were gone.
Now I was left to do my work and your many tasks—all alone.

"I'm sorry for not helping more," is a trite phrase,
Haunting me throughout solitary household days.
I miss many things you did as memories flash through.
I wish I was more thoughtful in supporting you—I am alone!

Frank, July 15, 2009

We had well-differentiated roles in our generation. Leanne took care of nurturing the family and managing our home. She was Queen of our castle. My role was to sally forth to slay dragons and to provide the resources necessary for the family. Now, I had to assume complete responsibility for both roles. For the first time, I learned just how skilled Leanne was in multitasking. I regretted that I could not thank her profusely for all of the countless little things she did without me realizing the magnitude of the tasks. I now recalled her comment, "If I pass first, who will keep your clothes neatly in the drawers and watch out for you?"

I remember Leanne's shock when she visited my room in the hospital where I worked as an emergency lab technician. She observed how I carelessly threw the socks in my drawer and saw clothes littering the room. She probably thought I would change. However, my sloppy habits never did! Regretfully, I relied on her exemplary neatness to compensate for my inherent carelessness.

I also reminisced about our life together in my daily letters, which I illustrated with pictures. These captured my moods of the day. However, poems gave me the greatest opportunity to pour out my thoughts. Some of these "folk poems" were mundane, like the one on housework; others were about our long relationship. Some appeared as God-given insights. As I reviewed the nightly letters in preparation for this chapter, I saw my slow progress out of despair and into an understanding of my new life. Slowly, ever so slowly, a new perspective formed.

It is amazing how the tincture of time changes the balance of the trivial and the important. My office was in our home and Leanne would come into my office and sit down to go over a topic that was important to her in the management of our household. I usually repressed my annoyance. After she passed, I took that chair out of my office because of the deep longing I had for those frequent interruptions.

I often attempted to express my thoughts about our life together in simple poems. For example, in my study, I have a large picture of Leanne between my desk and my theological library. One evening, I was dictating and swiveling in my desk chair looking at her picture. The reflection of the ceiling lights on the books formed shadows on the glass covering her picture. These appeared as silver and gold threads spinning in space. In an instant, that thought was of great comfort to me and led to the following poem that captured the hope of a new day.

When Silver and Gold Threads Reappear

You left faster than I thought on August 4th morn,
I held you and talked as you began to slip away that dawn,
The day was sunny — my heart was drenched with tears,
I desperately hoped I could hold you for years.

Nine months, you've been away; a long time.
Anguish, loneliness, and sadness stalk my mind.
But slowly dark clouds are beginning to pass away.
I'm observing a brilliant fabric emerge: possibly a new day.

As I look around our home and yard, I see you everywhere,
In the garden, in our bedroom, and in the empty chair.
A bit of physical and spiritual healing is taking place.
On your picture, silver and gold threads weave in space.

I cannot mourn for the previous fabric rent asunder
As you reside in my heart, I'm actively weaving another.
Magnificent silvery gold tapestry to last while I have life,
Centered and revolving around my Christ given wife.

Yes, you have departed to your heavenly home.
Nevertheless, I am not abandoned or alone,
God's overflowing grace is enabling my spirit to grow,
Assuring I'll see you again and your face I will know!

Frank, May 18, 2009

I am still processing a wide variety of emotions that are an amalgam of faith, loneliness, sorrow, and hope. I read books on grief, death, and heaven. I thought about the question in the first catechism, "What is the chief end of man?" Answer: "The chief end of man is to glorify God and enjoy him forever." I resumed reading my Bible, focusing on the books in the New Testament that had provided comfort in the past, beginning with the Gospels of John and Luke. Still, I found myself adrift. My relationship with God was sporadic and turbulent during the acute phase. However, I did not get angry with God since I was partially prepared for all of this when I dreamed that Leanne would pass first.

My prayer and devotional life left much to be desired. Mystified, I returned repeatedly to the question: Why did Leanne die before me, a person with chronic heart disease? It caused me to question how I should live and carry on. I sought to clarify my understanding of God's omnipotence and providential will. *I searched for a purpose for my remaining days and vainly tried to find the meaning of this unexpected turn of events.*

My devotions resumed toward the end of the acute phase, but I had great difficulty going to church because it evoked painful memories of Leanne's absence from worship, the center of our life. Our son Frank was extremely helpful. He quietly accompanied me to worship. Frequently, favorite hymns moved me to tears. As I look back now, I can see more clearly different *controlling* thought patterns emerging from the foundation that was laid during those first thirty days of solitude.

During my seclusion, I pondered whether I should keep a journal. I have mentioned before that I use a speech recognition program on the computer due to bilateral carpal tunnel syndrome, so I decided to journal in the form of spoken letters to Leanne. Initially, these letters were emotionally difficult and accompanied by tears.

These letters emerged, not only as a form of communication, but also as a way to continue to share my innermost feelings with Leanne. Yes, I was aware that it was a monologue, but it enabled me to "talk" through my turmoil and express my grief without judgment and anxiety. Eventually, I wrote to her daily. The last portion of the letter, dictated at night, was particularly comforting.

Leanne had requested that I develop a Sunday afternoon lunch fellowship for widowers. She emphasized that it was to be a time of fellowship without any Bible teaching. Initially, I thought it was just to be done as an outreach and service to others. I soon realized that Leanne knew that it would also prevent me from retreating into myself.

This fellowship for widowers revealed to me that I had many experiences in common with these men who had also become *suddenly single.* Each of us considered his wife to be the only love of his life. We all agreed that activity was important for keeping us in contact with others, and we each admitted that we talked to our wives around the house. We all took much comfort from our visits to the cemetery and we loved to share stories about our wives.

This fellowship provided a safe place where we could reveal our thoughts without the fear of judgment. It also enabled us to talk fondly about our wives and discuss the many gifts that they gave us through our marriages without the fear of boring everyone. We were "single men" helping each other deal with loss. This group continues to provide me with resources for coping with my grief.

True to form, I eventually controlled my grief by hurling myself back into work only to find the satisfaction I got from work was not what it was while Leanne was alive. Nevertheless, it was like occupational therapy in that it diverted my mind, consumed time, and kept me from wallowing in pity. It also generated the finances to pay for medical and funeral expenses, address family financial needs, and support our commitment to our church home.

At some point in our marriage, Leanne and I developed a tribal concept in which the family unit would function together to support each other in times of health crises, to overcome unusual financial difficulties, and to mentor, as appropriate, our children and grandchildren. Simply put, it was our responsibility to secure the next generations. In our discussions, we decided that, in addition to work as therapy, it would also be required to help meet our family's needs.

Yes, Leanne did insist that I go back to a full workload, but I overcompensated. In part, I had difficulty estimating my workload because I no longer had Leanne to help moderate my utilization of time. I never could estimate accurately how long it would take to complete a project. Now, in the midst of grief, my workload calculations were even more inaccurate. Nevertheless, the heavy work schedule forced me outside of myself and provided welcome nourishment by way of partner and board meetings. Furthermore, since Leanne had never been involved in these types of activities, they were more psychologically comfortable for me.

Emotionally difficult times remained. Sometimes my anguish would focus on a theme that I would eventually express in a simple, but meaningful rhyme. For example, I was distraught as our first anniversary apart approached. At those times, I would often look at pictures from yesteryear. For example, looking back on our marriage from the vantage point of our fifty-second anniversary, which I celebrated alone, the word *forever* leaped into my mind. From that word, the poem "Forever" (pg. 36) emerged as a word picture of my commitment to our continued love affair during my *single life*. It was a time of intense pain.

As I passed through this milestone of our first anniversary alone, it was apparent that pathological patterns were beginning to emerge. First, it became increasingly difficult to sleep, and I feared becoming dependent on Xanax. Second, I was beginning to cope by filling time with an unusually heavy work schedule. I also began to resent being in a crowd of happy people, because I remained in despair and they were enjoying life!

Throughout the beginning of this chronic phase, I attempted to control and manage my grief process in the same way that I was accustomed to managing activities in my sphere of work. My tendency to be a controlling person became more pronounced. My one great solace was writing poems and letters to Leanne. These were reflections of my struggles through the morass of grief.

Reflections

This is a very special sunny and utterly somber day.
I am reflecting on the eleven months since you went away.
Your last month of life must have been dreadful for you.
But together, we expressed our love and saw it through.

I tried my very best to make it pleasant and calm.
Holding my feelings inside and trying to be a balm.
But my tears came rushing through as fountains of love,
As I thought of your departure to heaven above.

I prayed as the month of July flew rapidly past.
For God to take you so you would have no more harm.
As pain began to grab you and pull your comfort away.
Through it, your love and faith remained strong and stayed.

The last morning when you gasped struggling for breath,
I saw firsthand your impending final battle with death.
I held you tightly as you labored with each rapid respiration.
Until peacefully you left me with anguishing tears of reflection.

Looking back my love has steadfastly grown.
We're apart in a way I never thought would be known.
Fearing I would leave first, I inflicted you with my ghost.
I know with certainty now it is God's plan we must trust.

Frank, July 4, 2009

Learning to Trust

I used the word *trust* in the last line of "Reflections," but I was not yet really trusting God with my whole life. I still grappled with grief, trying to understand the purpose of these unexpected extra years. Why did I not die first? Initially, I read books on grief, death, and heaven. Then my attention turned to various books of the Bible. However, no big picture emerged.

One day, I remembered a former pattern of Bible study that Dr. David Allen taught me in our bi-weekly lunches in his office. He recommended three major steps. First, read a single verse or a cluster of verses three times. Then, meditate on those verses for about twenty minutes. Finally, use those verses to form the foundation of spiritual contemplation throughout the day.

I began this format of study in the book of Ephesians every evening before going to sleep. While I was studying chapter four, the words *trust God* crashed into my consciousness. Those two words are not actually used in the fourth chapter, but I pondered whether they could be a gift from the Holy Spirit. I meditated on those two words and wrote my thoughts about them in my letter to Leanne on Aug. 17, 2009.[13]

---

[13] Reading of the Scripture, one verse a day, followed by meditation followed by contemplation has really made me realize I was not trusting God as I should. I now know more fully what you meant by, "Is it wrong to have so much joy?" I think you were struggling with the concept of whether it should be joyful to leave this life and go to be with the Lord. I don't think I was angry with God for taking you sooner than I ever expected, but instead, I was trying to deal with my grief by controlling it rather than trusting God. I have been contemplating repeatedly what it means to trust God. While it is hard to put into words, I guess it means that I need to turn over all control to our Lord and Savior. As I began to do that, an unusual sense of peace settled in my life. Yes, I long to see you, yet I realize that heaven is not merely for reuniting with love ones who've gone before, but for the worship of our Father, the appreciation of our Savior's grace, and the guidance of the Holy Spirit. Even when I did not realize it, He was active in my life. For the very first time, I feel God filling the emptiness in my life. It does not mean that I do not miss you and long for you, but instead of only the pain and suffering of grief, God has provided peace. I know you will be pleased because, in our conversations, you wanted me to be able to go on and I promised you that I would. Nevertheless, I have been walking this past year through life in a joyless state. This new approach to Scripture made me realize that I was trying to live my life in my own strength.

Then, in a rapid stream of consciousness, I dictated the poem "Trust God." This epiphany was the beginning of my journey to the other side of grief. It was still to take many months, but a major change had occurred! As I wrote, the reality of my self-pity plunged into my being like a knife. I realized that grief was a response to profound loss. Grief left me emotionally rudderless in a turbulent sea of sadness and loneliness. The descent into despair was also accompanied by self-pity rather than gratitude for fifty-one years of marriage. A gift I never expected!

Trust God

Trusting God is such a simple phrase.
Its complexity escaped me for many days,
Until I began to realize who is in control.
God then spoke and enabled me to understand my role.

It was through Scripture, meditation and contemplation,
That I began to understand life turns and temptations.
The ultimate sin is self-attempting to control one's destiny,
And understanding to rely on God is fact not fantasy.

Idolatry takes many forms in the world today.
Not dumb stone statues bending my pathway,
Instead, it was my narcissistic self-centered life,
Denying me God's peace, leaving me empty without wife.

I thought it was grief that stole my heartfelt zest for life.
Dark feelings of loneliness filled my morning and night.
So I embarked on busyness, controlling most of the day.
Until God shattered my pride by teaching to trust and abide.

Those profound simple words "Trust God" will stay,
Reverberating within my mind throughout the day.
Providing a peace that eluded me this past year,
Now enabling me to go on humbly in trust, not fear.
                                    Frank, August 17, 2009

I am still not exactly sure where I am in this journey, but I do know that a peace and equanimity has finally begun to displace my self-pity and idolatry. I did not realize how much God could work in my heart. It was as if I had seen a new land after a voyage on turbulent seas. I was about to enter the country named "The

Other Side of Grief." Simply put, *I had to let go of managing Leanne's loss and let God restore hope in my life!*

What do I mean by the other side of grief? To understand this complex phenomenon, I meditated on the process of grief which has caused me to further ponder the defining seminal moments in human life. I am just beginning to grasp the mystery of conception, birth, development, marriage, child rearing, maturing years, and the fading of one's faculties until death opens the door to heaven. I postulate that life can be reduced to seven major phases.

1. First, a fertilized egg is implanted in the mother's womb rather than being lost within the menstrual flow.

2. Second, a remarkable synchronizing develops the fertilized egg into a fully formed baby by a variety of genetic and chemical interactions. During the in utero gestation, the baby passes through numerous hazardous phases. Infections, toxins, and drugs can interrupt the normal process of development.

3. Third, is a journey through the birth canal. Each baby is formed through the development of a fertilized egg containing a set of genes passed down through generations. It enters the world after a dangerous pressure-filled journey through a birth canal. Following the cutting of the cord, the baby finds itself in an unwanted environment. These monumental physiological changes must be successfully navigated so that the newborn can live independently in a dependent fashion.

4. Fourth, there is the nurturing home where the baby receives the early imprint of its environment. Later, there is an awakening of the quest for understanding of the seminal questions: Who am I? Why am I here? Where am I going? These questions dawn slowly on us. Yet, in the first few years of one's life, many of one's patterns for dealing with the world are formed by outside and inside influences that are largely unappreciated. By nine years of age, most of the fundamental coping skills and interests are defined and the remaining time in childhood and adolescence is devoted to understanding how to adapt these early experiences to an adult world.

5. Fifth, there is a decision whether to marry, mate, propagate a family, or remain single. This decision will define and shape a large measure of one's adult life and responsibilities.

6. Sixth, and most important, is whether one is "born again." By that, I mean whether the individual receives and responds to the call of God. The answer to that question will define whether a person's Worldview is theistic, atheistic, or agnostic.

7. Seventh, the inevitable consequence of life is death followed by the transition to eternity.

As I contemplated these seven facts, I realized how much one's defining moments involve singleness. Conception, development, birth, childhood, second birth, and death are all events that a person experiences singularly. I began to see that, while I grieved that Leanne went into eternity before I did, marriage to this magnificent, beautiful woman was a great blessing. I had a profound awareness that the anticipation of dying after some twenty years of married life produced an overwhelming sense of gratitude for our fifty-one-years of life together.

Now that Leanne was in heaven, I tried to imagine from various images in the Bible what heaven would be like. I realized that only someone who had been there and who came to earth could accurately describe Leanne's heavenly home. That *someone* was Jesus Christ. Furthermore, a spurious thought influenced this view that has taken on greater meaning as I contemplated these seven stages, especially stages one and two. It began with a query: If one was in a single place for nine months, would that person remember anything about it? Most people to whom I addressed this question replied, "Of course." The follow-up question is, "What do you remember about your nine months in utero?" The answer was uniformly, "Nothing!"

Death is the final mystery, the final transition in life. The answers to questions about the nature of death and its aftermath are found only in the Bible. The most succinct answer comes from the pen of St. Paul, "To be absent from the body is to be present with the Lord" (2 Cor. 5:8). Other Scriptures provide further insight. However, it is hard to fully comprehend or even partially understand what happens after death.

These thoughts about *singularity* in no way diminish the incredibly fulfilling joy of the *oneness* of marriage. They are simply two different concepts. Genesis 2:24-25 states, "For this reason a man will leave his father and mother and be united to his wife and they will become one flesh. The man and his wife were both naked and they felt no shame." Physical nakedness is natural within the bonds of marriage as two people come to accept each other's body. But the emotional nakedness that must accompany a true union is much more difficult.

When it is achieved, however, that union is a remarkable blessing. It ushers in an entirely different relationship in which two independent "singularities" join together by pledging all that they have to each other. This brief exchange of vows ends with the words, "...until death do you part." The joy experienced by two people who are equally yoked is a true gift from God.

As I moved deeper into the *Land on the Other Side of Grief,* I began to understand that much of my earlier thoughts were not sorrow for Leanne's death, but pity, a relentless self-pity, for the unexpected change that occurred in my own life. I was no longer able to enjoy the same companionship, our intimate passion, our parenting, being Grammy and Gramps together, our many deep discussions, our worship, and our devotional time as a couple. I miss our relationship immensely. Life will never be the same!

Part of my longing for Leanne grows out of the overwhelming burden of assuming both of our roles in all aspects of family life. The adjustment was profound. God's grace carried me unwittingly to a new place where I could enjoy the richness of our marriage and be confident in my new deeper relationship with Jesus. This provided a peace that passes all human understanding. Now, I experienced Leanne's life verse (Phil. 4:6-7) in a deeper and profound way. My own life verse, Romans 8:38-39, also took on a new meaning. I had many more steps to take in the *Land on the Other Side of Grief,* but I had arrived on a different shore.

As I contemplated our wedding ceremony, I meditated on the vows we took and on the weddings which I had attended or presided over as a pastor. On the second wedding anniversary without Leanne, I pondered the statement, "Til death do you part." I tried to understand how these words applied to us now. As those words reverberated in my mind, a poem emerged.

Till Death Do You Part

Fifty-three years have passed since you walked down the aisle.
I stood dazzled by your beauty and beheld you with a broad smile.
Later you confided in me with overflowing love in your heart,
You knew from my countenance that we would never part.

Those unusual words in the wedding ceremony's query,
Seemed so far away that we would never have to face a dreary
Moment when one of us would depart from this tiny sphere,
Leaving the other in solitude, filled with overwhelming tears.

Contemplating those words uttered fifty-three years ago,
I realized that they were merely a permission to go
On with one's life in whatever the fashion.
To rekindle on Earth another loving passion.

It was not a requirement to part someday.
There is another option that comes each person's way.
To remain grounded in a marriage of complete blended passion
And to begin a forward-looking life rooted in this splendid fashion.

So my dear, what am I saying on this anniversary milestone?
Simply, my vows of fidelity and commitment to our goals are honed.
I will implement each agreement made during our earthly travels.
Continuing with you in my being: our relationship has not unraveled.

I realize now that death is merely a transition phase of life.
It's not to be feared or postponed by medicine at all cost.
Life is not something through the dying process that is lost,
Tis the beginning of a new phase of God's plan forecast.

My love for you is not some fading short-lived ember.
It burns yearly from October to the next coming September.
As brightly as the day when we first mingle with each other,
And promise our love through eternity to one another.

Frank, October 20, 2009

I became overwhelmingly thankful for the woman with whom I had the privilege of sharing my life for fifty-one years. I was blessed to have married a woman of faith who was honest, industriousness, compassionate, nurturing, sincere, forthright, and strong. Leanne was a caring mother, a supportive grandmother, and a Christian witness. She was truly a "Proverbs 31 woman." I could trust her with all that I was and ever would be. Her legacy will continue throughout the generations.

Finally, her steadfast faith in the face of death blessed me. I can appreciate more than ever the grace of Jesus as she trod steadfastly on a path which she did not choose. During this phase of her life, she gave us more gifts of herself than I could ever describe. It was through her journey, her transition in death, that I realized that I loved her more in those last three-plus months than ever before in our married life. My vision is that we remain married—one dwelling in heaven and the other on earth.

Uttered Words and Meditations of Heart
A meditation on Psalm 19

The amazing patterns of speech we utter.
Emanate from neuronal connections and flutters
Transmitted by acetylcholine in nanoseconds of time.
These thoughts course quickly through the mind.

The words cascade sometimes in a thoughtless flow.
From the locked recesses of consciousness we know,
In reality shaped by discourse of agreed-upon words,
To those who will receive them in patterns on the go.

Meditation combines these random discordant utterances,
Into a meaningful, vibrantly colored picture of reality around,
The essence of the concepts designed to be conveyed
Into a comprehensive motivational action to be purveyed.

Thus the combination of words and deep emotion
Merge to form the foundation of an individual's devotion.
A communication in communion with our celestial God
Providing meaning to this life that will end in earthly sod.

Yet, absent from the body is present with the Lord
Encourages and guides our wanderings on our earthly abode.
Providing a Worldview for the travels through joys and pains,
The Rock, our salvation gives purposeful meaning for life ever again.

Frank, December 22, 2010

Lessons Learned

1. The chronic phase of grief requires reflection on one's marital life, working through unfinished business, and undergoing a huge transition to singleness. One must reconcile a variety of discordant emotions such as disappointment, anger, anxiety, depression, and survivor's guilt.

2. It is likely that a long bonded relationship will result in a prolonged journey through "Grief City" in the land of grieving (see page 167). Unfortunately, some people do not reach the *Land on the Other Side of Grief.*

3. Understanding one's relationship to God is the most essential part of the journey to the *Land on the Other Side of Grief.*

4. In the early phases of grief, both men and women are likely to disregard their health needs, especially if they lose the joy of living. It is important to note there is a high incidence of death of the surviving partner within two years of the death of the spouse. Nutrition, exercise, and routine preventive care are essential for both physical and mental health. Guarding against lethargy is particularly important for men, who tend to retreat into isolation following the loss of a beloved wife.

5. Social activity is essential to overcome the isolation that accompanies the loss of a spouse. This may be in the form of continued work, community events, or family interaction.

   Those who have been recently widowed may be sought out, consciously or unconsciously, by other widows or widowers. *Suddenly single* women significantly outnumber their male counterparts. Vulnerability is high during this chronic stage of grief because the grieving spouse must suddenly supply so many of the mundane needs of life that were once fulfilled by the departed spouse.

6. This can lead to prematurely entering into a romantic relationship. When considering remarriage, remember that the phrase in the wedding vows, "til death do you part," is an option, it is not a command.

5

Crossing to the Land
on the Other Side of Grief

Death is not unusual. People die every day. But each death is unique.
Lives woven together are now torn apart.[14]

Grief is a basic emotion that occurs throughout human life. It varies in intensity from disappointment to profound despair and emptiness. *An acute loss, whether it is a friendship, a job, a cherished possession, or the death of a friend, icon, or loved one, evokes these feelings of loss. Only the depth of grief varies.* The degree of grief is also influenced by the perception of the object or person that is lost, one's relationship to the departed, and the culture in which one lives. One of the greater molding influences is the family's interpretation of and response to significant loss, whether it is a person, position, or possession. The depth and length of one's grief is defined by the relationship of the grieving person to the one who has suddenly died or separated by a divorce or broken relationship. The characteristics of how we grieve are defined primarily by one's Worldview.

> Bereavement is a universal and integral part of our experience of love. It follows marriage as normally as marriage follows courtship or as autumn follows summer. It is not a truncation of the process but one of its phases; not an interruption of the dance, but the next figure. —C. S. Lewis

Theologically, there are three major Worldviews: theistic, agnostic, and atheistic. The agnostic denial of death is illustrated by the Simon and Garfunkel song "Flowers Never Bend with the Rainfall," cited earlier. Existential nihilism is among the fuller expressions of this view and one of the many expositors of this view, Shakespeare's *Macbeth*, expresses it most poetically:

---

[14] Susan. J. Zonnebelt and Robert. C. Vries, *Getting to the Other Side of Grief: Overcoming the Loss of a Spouse*, Baker Books, 1998, pg. 9.

Out, out, brief candle!
Life's but a walking shadow, a poor player
That struts and frets his hour upon the stage
And then is heard no more; it is a tale
Told by an idiot, full of sound and fury,
Signifying nothing.

The first and last stanzas quoted from William Henley's poem "Invictus" illustrate an atheistic stoicism:

Out of the night that covers me,
Black as the Pit from pole to pole,
I thank whatever gods may be
For my unconquerable soul.

It matters not how strait the gate,
How charged with punishments the scroll.
I am the master of my fate:
I am the captain of my soul.

The apostle Paul expresses a theistic view of the relationship between a child of God and Christ in Romans 8:38-39:

> For I am persuaded that neither death nor life, neither angels nor principalities, neither the present nor the future, nor any powers neither height nor depth, nor anything else in all creation, will be able to separate us from the love of God that is in Christ Jesus our Lord.

The journeys in this chapter reflect a Christian Worldview. After being a midwife in my wife's death and passage to the next world, I began to understand that controlling grief was a form of idolatry. I was driven to let go and trust God for the remainder of my life. I was about to cross into a different place.

A Tour of the Landscape

The acute and chronic phases of my grief were like a sea of crashing emotions. There were waves with high crests and troughs of turbulence through which my mind spun endlessly without direction. Then, through eventually trusting God, it was as if I landed on the shore of a different land, which I will name for the purpose of this book the *Land on the Other Side of Grief*. Many of my selfish, self-centered feelings of despair and loss diminished. I ceased pitying my plight within that terrible endless dark hole of grief. My life was being filled by the presence of God. I began to realize, as expressed by C. S. Lewis, that the death of a partner in a marriage was the logical outcome of a bonded life.

Every marriage inevitably separates by death or divorce or some other form of abandonment. I also realized the profound nature of the gift of Leanne's life and my thankfulness for a longer marriage to her than I ever expected. This insight engendered a new sense of peace. My understanding ushered in a deeper phase of bondedness. Yes, loneliness and sorrow punctuated these seasons of life, but they were replaced by an ever-growing appreciation of the gift of salvation that God granted and the very essence of our oneness in a Christ-centered marriage. Furthermore, I was comforted that the Scriptures teach that we believers do not cease to exist upon death. Death is merely a phase transition. Note the experience of Gary Habermas in the aftermath of his wife's death.[15]

I can best illustrate the nature of bondedness and the stages of romance, engagement, marriage, and the growing bonds that unite a man and a woman through this simple homespun poem. It describes my emotions upon meeting Leanne for the first time. It also describes my emerging view of our continuing love affair which began in medical school when I noticed an exceptionally efficient and beautiful nurse, who worked on the seventh floor of Memorial Hospital. It was Leanne! Bonding to her was, as the title of the poem says, "As Natural as Leaves to a Tree." And now, in the final stanza of my life, "The tree is now much older and part of it is gone / But the remaining leaves hold tight and strong."

---

[15] "Throughout, the single, most healing thought for me was a personal assurance that God had raised his Son from the dead. Many a time I sat on the front porch and contemplated the truth of this event. While this might seem beside the point for some, I realized that, as long as this was a world where Jesus was raised from the grave, not only was I assured that I would see my wife again for eternity, but further, I did not have to know *why* she died. The resurrection shows that God was in control, even when I did not understand. She was safe with him, and I was totally convinced that she would not have returned, even if she had the opportunity. Internalizing this truth brought me profound healing, even during the summer she died." G.R. Habermas and J. P. Moreland, *Beyond Death: Exploring the Evidence for Immortality*, Crossway Books, Good News Publishers, 1998, pg. 355.

As Natural as Leaves to a Tree

The night was calm and the hospital was still,
When I first saw you and believed I was ill,
Because my heart left me and took flight,
Bonding to you as naturally as leaves to a tree.

Our conversations must have lasted two hours or more.
As I stumbled unwittingly through a very large door,
Into a new romantic world that I never knew before.
I had found the woman who I would forever adore.

How could I capture this beautiful industrious nurse?
Who chilled February's ardor when I asked for a date,
By a demurely uttered "NO" coming as a sudden dark curse,
Yet the request of a "rain check" emboldened my fright!

I had to conquer uncertainty and fear of rebuff.
Did I misread the signals because love blinded sight?
As a moth drawn uncontrollably to a bright light,
I called to see if another arrangement, could, maybe, might?

As I struggled for words, something must have come out right.
We went to a student infested grill on campus Saturday night.
Conversation darted from topics like rolling waters through lilies.
Tumbling over rocks of faith, family, life values—I knew she's for me.

Conspiring relentlessly to pursue this lovely young lass,
I awkwardly tried to kiss her on our first lovely date: bad pass!
She gently pushed me away — did rejection seal my fate?
Confused I returned to my room: was I too late?

Later learning her values of propriety ruled that first night
I crafted a plan to win her heart as in four months we'd part.
Steadfastly, but not hastily, before internship's barrier in July,
We agreed in June to be engaged: wed till one would die.

She set the date for October 20th: a splendid fall day.
The leaves on our separate trees were colored and gay
As we exchanged our vows and said I do,
A new tree began to grow and bud before you.

For fifty-one years the tree prospered and grew,
Limbs aged but the leaves held true.
When sunny days, winds and storms came through,
Until that August day when I temporarily lost you.

The tree is now much older and part of it is gone.
But the remaining leaves hold tight and strong.
To the steady trunk that was born that long ago day.
Watching seedlings growing, each in their own way

Frank, February 11, 2010

This new state of singleness is analogous to a shipwrecked individual tossed benevolently onto the shore of a new land. It was as if I yielded to the force of the sea and was carried tenderly ashore. It was a new and unfamiliar landscape. Although there continued to be struggles with the past forms of idolatry and of control, I was no longer wallowing in the depths of self-pity. A new dawn appeared based on the realization that life was to be lived even though loneliness would persist.

I began to have a deeper appreciation of the gift of a cherished loved one who is missing for a season. A new understanding of the very essence of marriage began to dawn. As I read God's Word about marriage between a man and a woman, I began to realize different facets of our life that were now blooming in the garden of reality. Respect is the greatest gift a man and woman can receive from each other: "However, each one of you also must love his wife as he loves himself, and the wife must respect her husband" (Eph. 5:33).

Respect

In the quest for self, we see mirrors in other's eyes,
Searching to understand the meaning of our lives.
Love is a bond that binds us to God and to each other.
I crave respect from my wife: she knows me more than my mother.

As God clearly teaches in His clarion Word.
Man must love wife like self and certainly above others.
Giving himself to sustain her and as Christ did the Church.
Man cannot sanctify, but he can love her as they become one.

I have been blessed by ceaseless respect from my wife.
She nurtured, supported, and honored me throughout her life.
Though she is now gone to Glory with our Savior above,
Her respect and my earthly adoration, unites us in God's love
Frank, August 18, 2009

I was often perplexed by Leanne's query, as she was passing, "Is it wrong to have so much joy?" I always replied, "No," but I was afraid to ask what she meant. As I read the First Epistle of John, I concluded that she was experiencing this joy of fellowship with God as she prepared to pass from this world to the next.

That which was from the beginning, we have heard, which we have seen with our eyes, which we have looked upon and our hands have touched—this we proclaim concerning the Word of life. The life appeared; we have seen and testify to it, and we proclaim to you the eternal life, which was with the Father and has appeared to us. We proclaim to you what we have seen and heard, so that you may have fellowship with us. And our fellowship is with the Father and his Son, Jesus Christ. And these things we write to you to make our joy complete. —1 Jn. 1:1-4

Leanne's life's verse, Philippians 4:6-7, provided the peace that accompanied this joy. Yes, there were still pangs of loneliness that crescendoed periodically at holidays and special times such as birthdays and family gatherings, but they were also accompanied by gratitude and pleasant memories.

On December 19, 2010, we were at church singing "Oh, Come, All Ye Faithful." As the congregation was singing, tears began to flow down my face. I do not know why, but I was suddenly quite sad. Then an odd thing occurred while singing the second verse: "Sing choirs of angels, sing in exultation, *oh, sing, all ye bright hosts of heaven above!* Glory to God. All glory in the highest!"

When I got to the italicized words, I had a flashing vision of Leanne singing with the heavenly hosts. I could not tell how she was clothed, but she appeared to be in a white garment. I could see her face clearly. She was younger than when she died and appeared extraordinarily happy as she sang with the choir. I tried to hold onto the vision, but it left before we got to the chorus. My tears of sadness turned to gladness. I was dumbfounded. I could only conclude that this was either a neural aberration, or, as I believe, I was given a brief glimpse of heaven. It was like that old hymn "Heaven Came Down and Glory Fill My Soul." I marveled at this vision and I treasured it. It changed my whole outlook for the day and throughout the Christmas season.

Paths of Grief

Each pilgrim must blaze fresh paths in this *Land on the Other Side of Grief*. I realized early on that my own paths of grief were going to be tortuous, difficult, and winding. They rise and fall and crisscross back and forth like bunny trails. But just when the going seems to be too much for me, God leads me to a refreshing spring where I find the inspiration to go on. One such source of encouragement is *The Pilgrim's Progress from This World to That Which is to Come* by John Bunyan. I am particularly struck by Christian's description of climbing the Hill of Difficulty:

> Christian now went to the spring, and drank thereof to refresh himself, and then began to go up the hill saying,
>
> The Hill, though high I covet to ascend,
> The difficulty will not me offend;
> For I perceive the Way to Life lies here.
> Come, pluck up heart, let's neither faint nor fear!
> Better, though difficult, the right way to go,
> Then wrong, though easy where the end is woe.[16]

There are many paths in this new land and each must forge his or her own way to make sense of this new *suddenly single* state. Essentially, each of us will combine old patterns with the new challenges on this journey. I hope that a few illustrations of the common paths that people have taken will encourage you. You are not alone.

Some may have experienced such profound loss that they remain at sea a long time and perhaps never escape the clutches of grief. Horatio Spafford and his wife, Anna, lost their four-year-old son to scarlet fever in 1870. The great Chicago Fire of 1871 brought financial devastation to the Spaffords. Horatio had invested heavily in real estate on the shores of Lake Michigan and the fire burned every one of his properties to the ground.

In an attempt to heal from these tragedies, Horatio and Anna planned to take their four daughters to Britain to join D. L. Moody on an evangelistic campaign. Just before sailing from New York, Horatio was called back to Chicago on business. Not wanting to disappoint his family, he told them to go on without him and he would join them soon. Nine days later their ship, the *Ville Du Havre*, and the *Lochearn* collided at sea and 246 of the 303 passengers and crew perished. Among the lost were the Spaffords' four daughters. Anna's now famous telegram to her husband read only, "Saved alone." In the aftermath of this tragic collision,

---

[16] John Bunyan, *The Pilgrim's Progress from This World to That Which Is to Come*: Samuel Bagster and Sons, London, 1845, pg. 31.

Horatio Spafford wrote the famous poem "It Is Well with My Soul"[17] which was set to music by Philip Bliss who himself died three years later in a train accident. The words and music have been a comfort to many through the years:

1. When peace, like a river, attendeth my way,
    When sorrows like see billows roll;
    Whatever my lot, thou hast taught me to say,
    It is well, it is well, with my soul.

    (Refrain)
    It is well, with my soul,
    It is well, it is well, with my soul.

2. Though Satan should buffet, though trials should come,
    Let this blessed assurance control,
    That Christ has regarded my helpless estate,
    And hath shed his own blood for my soul.

3. My sin, oh, the bliss of this glorious thought!
    My sin not in part but the whole,
    Is nailed to the cross, and I bear it no more,
    Praise the Lord, praise the Lord, all my soul!

4. And Lord, haste the day when my faith shall be sight,
    The clouds be rolled back as a scroll;
    The trump shall resound, and the Lord shall descend,
    Even so, it is well with my soul.

This was not the end of their journey of grief. As Horatio and his wife searched for meaning and understanding in these tragic events, their life was complicated further when he was expelled by his home church. The expulsion was for a lack of belief in hell and a personal devil, and for believing that innocent children, including their own, would not be sent to hell for eternity.[18] The death of their four daughters at sea, the loss of their only son, Horatio Jr., to scarlet fever, Horatio's business losses from the Chicago Fire, and their expulsion from the church lead to

---

[17] Bertha Spafford Vester, *Our Jerusalem: An American Family in the Holy City*, 1841-1949: Doubleday & Company, Garden City, N.Y., 1950, pg. 46.

[18] Ibid., pg. 56.

recriminations from others similar to those Job received from his "friends." People concluded that they must have sinned to have had such catastrophes. The nasty press reports[19] led the Spaffords and some other people of the Lake View Fellowship to embark for the Holy Land on August 17, 1881.

In Jerusalem, the American colony began to serve the downtrodden and poor of all faiths. In the summer of 1888, Horatio Spafford died of malignant malaria and his wife continued the work he started. The journey of this family of faith and their descendants in the *Land on the Other Side of Grief* continued until 1947. The colony, born out of tragedy, bigotry, prejudice, and misunderstanding, served the poor of Christian, Jewish, and Muslim faith communities through two world wars. Members of the colony lived to see the establishment of the state of Israel. The Spaffords' journey on the path to the *Land on the Other Side of Grief* was confounded by many difficulties, but through it all they found *a new purpose born out of tragedy!*

Others in this *Land on the Other Side of Grief* may wander on a path that leads to a new relationship that may culminate in remarriage. Susan Zonnebelt-Smeenge and Robert C. De Vries describe in detail their experience as a grieving psychologist and a grieving pastor wandering in the *Land on the Other Side of Grief.*[20] Their story is instructive as it chronicles the formation of a new relationship based initially on friendship. These authors also describe a general condition for the different experiences of grieving that occur in men and women. As a metaphor, they posit that the second marriage after the death of a spouse is more like a corporate merger due to the complexities of children, in-laws, wealth, and possessions that are simply not factors when two young people marry for the first time. Of course, there is a history of the previous bonded relationship as well.

---

[19] Ibid., pg. 58. A singular sect of Christians which has arisen in the northern suburbs of Chicago is known as the "Overcomers." They believe in personal inspiration, in direct communication with God, and the literal rendering of the Scriptures as applied to mundane affairs, and the future salvation of the universe including the devil. A party under the leadership of Mr. Spafford is about to go to Jerusalem to build up ruined places.

[20] Susan. J. Zonnebelt and Robert C. De Vries. *Getting to the Other Side of Grief: Overcoming the Loss of a Spouse*, Baker Books, Grand Rapids, Mich., Twelfth Printing, 2007, pg. 111-142.

Newlyweds in a first marriage usually start out with minimal possessions and forge their own bonded relationship. In the case of Susan and Robert, the subsequent marriage did not result in the abandonment of the memories of their former spouses, but they posited that people who have a happy marriage are more prepared to enter a new marital relationship based on the richness of their former marriage. Neither was looking for a new marital partner. Romance occurred in the course of their journey as friends. It began by helping each other through the process of grief. Their journey culminated in the writing of a book.[21] Chapter nine in their book focuses on the pros and cons of remarriage and the many facets to consider when contemplating remarriage while journeying in the *Land on the Other Side of Grief*. In other cases, I have seen men rapidly remarry, in part, to fill the void of loneliness. Some of these marriages ended tragically.

Challenges in the Land on the Other Side of Grief

Men, in particular, face a number of practical problems upon becoming *suddenly single*. For example, men born in the late twenties, thirties, and forties before there was more sharing of domestic responsibilities are likely to have limited ability to provide for their practical needs. Wives born in those years did the food preparation, housecleaning, laundry, and grocery shopping. Many wives of that era managed the family finances, the calendar of birthdays, anniversaries, and gifts. Such a wife is like the CEO of a kind of small family business in which the husband has little experience or interest.

Then there is a loss of intimacy and sexual outlet. While men and women have both intimacy and sexual needs, it is generally true that the loss of intimacy is more of an issue for women and loss of sexual outlet is a greater issue for men. *Sudden celibacy* may be very challenging for the *suddenly single*. One also experiences an immediate change in the relationships with friends who previously related to them as a couple. I found this to be particularly difficult. Not only was it hard for me to relate to a couple that we were close friends with, but other couples were experiencing their own grieving and did not know how to relate to my grief in the midst of their own.

---

[21] Susan. J. Zonnebelt and Robert. C. Vries, ibid., pg. 181-215.

The loss of a parent may change the way children relate to the surviving spouse. From observing other widowers and their families, I have noted a role reversal that is more rapid than the normal "parenting" role that children assume as their parents grow older. In these cases, children take on more responsibility for the grieving spouse which can be accompanied by resentment of this reverse parenting.

New and different competitions can also emerge among the siblings which add to the stress of the grieving spouse. All of these complex interrelationships must be sorted out during the journey in this *Land on the Other Side of Grief*. My greatest admonition is to allow yourself time for walking along a variety of paths before making major modifications in your life such as moving, establishing new relationships, dating, or withdrawal from normal patterns. Above all, it is important not to become a "hermit" by withdrawing from society. Church activities, grief counseling, community activities, and work may engage one's energies following a major disruption in the normal patterns of married life.

The health of the surviving spouse influences this journey significantly. Most widowers and widows experience high levels of depressive symptoms for up to two years. A comprehensive analysis of the health of the elderly is presented in the Health and Retirement Study.[22] Some men, after examining their own mortality in the aftermath of a wife's death, may conclude that remarriage to a younger woman will provide security and health care. However, explore these options very carefully.

In my ministry to widowers, I have found a number of men who choose to remain single. I count myself among them. As I wandered in this land, I reached a number of decisions based in large measure on the discussions Leanne and I had prior to her death. Although we gave each other the permission to remarry, we mutually concluded that we did not wish to do so. The decision to remain single for the rest of my life has shaped my path in this new land. After careful consideration and prayer, I concluded that I had the only love that I wish to have. I simply do not ever wish to have another woman disturb my love affair with Leanne. This is a

---

[22]http://www.nia.nih.gov/ResearchInformation/ExtramuralPrograms/Behavior alAndSocialResearch/HRSfull.htm

complex decision because I worried whether or not I was unduly hanging on to Leanne's memory. Was I able to go on with my life without her? The answer is a muted yes. As I describe in the Epilogue, I discovered a new ministry that has become my passion.

Clearly, my life must continue in her absence. I must regain my spiritual foothold in a new way. We could no longer have our devotions together, but I could include the devotions in the daily letter to Leanne when I woke up in the morning or at some other time during the day. I also needed to become self-sufficient with regard to personal requirements. This necessitated acquiring domestic skills, which I never possessed. Because I still work full time, I needed to obtain some help in performing the domestic work as well as the yard work. This trial and error process is still not perfect. I also realized that our children had lives of their own and I could not burden them or cling to them.

Fortunately, Leanne and I had a chance to discuss what I should do after her death. As mentioned earlier, she recommended that I begin a fellowship ministry for widowers, host the young married couple's class luncheon on a monthly basis and support the pastor in an advisory capacity. Leanne also strongly urged me to go back to work full time. By continuing to work, I could meet some family financial needs and aid in the education of our grandchildren and great grandchildren. Most importantly, work forced me to be engaged in "safe" social activities, thereby precluding my natural tendency to retreat into myself.

Conversations with men who have decided to remain single led me to believe that these men have also elected to have just one deep love. Of course, this commitment is modulated by the age of the person and other support systems that provide spiritual, social, and meaningful personal relationships. Many of these men find comfort in visiting the cemetery, sharing stories about their wives, and participating in vibrant family relationships. Social activities in church, discussion groups, and senior citizen clubs have been particularly meaningful to some. Each developed, or were developing, a path in the *Land on the Other Side of Grief*. The path is personal, unique, and provides meaning in the winter of their lives. Some even passed through winter to a new spring that enables the single man to appreciate the past and yet to enjoy new endeavors. In this *Land on the Other Side of Grief*, only one thing is inevitable—change!

The Land on the Other Side of Grief

Approaching the third anniversary of Thanksgiving alone,
I realize the Land on the Other Side of Grief is home.
The self-pity and yearning for something that cannot be,
Is being replaced by gratitude for the gifts you gave me.

In my study while talking to you, I realize life is not through.
God is healing the hole in my heart with insights anew.
I did not know in bitter days He was close by my side,
Teaching me His Grace as I am learning how to abide.

Yes, I still miss you in family gatherings and all that I do.
Reflecting on many years together married to you,
I know you would want me to go on with our Lord,
Where He takes me on Earth until my work is through.

In this new "Land" I am not sure I can clearly see,
The road ahead that is laid out for mortals like me,
But this I know without a doubt or a fear,
I can accept anything ahead, if He is near.
Frank, November 21, 2010

I am more conscious now than ever before of my dependence on God. I have an overwhelming gratitude for the life I shared with Leanne, the joy of our family adventures, and the many professional mountains that she enabled me to climb through her steadfast loving counsel and support.

Strategies for Coping with the Journey

As with any journey, one must have an objective and a perspective of the current situation. Making a list may be a good way to assess one's current condition. It may be helpful to understand one's destination and the need to acquire new skills for survival during this journey. For me, one of the most important requirements was to understand the nature of the journey. As a Christian, I searched to comprehend the meaning of this single life. I sought answers through prayer, meditation, contemplation, and Bible study. This was not an easy task. At times, I heard nothing. It was as if the heavens were brass!

In fact, at times, I wondered whether my life had any meaning now. Even though much of the acute anxiety and pain diminished,

I could not imagine what I could contribute without Leanne. These thoughts haunted me as I was traveling to Europe for a meeting. In one of my introspective moments, I wrote an email to my closest scientific colleague, Dr. Gary Wilson. We were so similar in our thinking patterns that we could even complete each other's sentences. His immediate response led to the following poem. It gave me new insight for my role in the family.

The Rock and the Glue

As I was traveling to Germany, I was very blue,
I missed you profoundly during the trip and knew,
That our romance would continue but separate in space,
I must gaze at pictures on walls and images to see your face.

In response to my email Gary Wilson answered with a reply,
You were the glue that bound our family together and did tie,
All of us tightly within your boundless faith and love,
That could only be given to you in an emanation from above.

He said that I was the rock on which the family must stand.
He posited that they still need me to be solid providing a hand,
When trouble arises, emotional crises appear, or finances crumble.
I must provide a solid foundation that withstands Earth's rumbles.

So we have filled so many roles as rock and glue,
Bound together with Christ in the center as we always knew,
No matter the challenge we faced, our faith would get us through.
Glue holding the family in bonds on a bedrock of life: me and you
Frank, June 10, 2009

I realized that I must still play a major leadership role within our family. I adopted the saying, "As long as one of us is here, both of us are." Therefore, I assumed both roles and, in so doing, I became acutely aware of how much Leanne held the family together. Now I had to do it for both of us! This role provided great joy. Occasionally our daughters even called me with questions they previously asked their mother.

Spiritual direction returned as I drew closer to God through Bible study, meditation, and contemplation in a verse-by-verse study. I resumed the pattern of Bible study, prayer, and hymn singing that formed the foundation of our devotions during our earthly marriage. Finally, I was able to participate wholeheartedly again in the worship services at church as a single person, but remembering our bond in Christian service throughout our lives.

The domestic chores were much more difficult. Leanne managed the entire home. I found it overwhelming to both work and manage smoothly all of the activities of a home. I was humbled to learn how arduous it was for single mothers to juggle family, home, and work. My workdays were long and, because sleep was difficult, I worked late into the night. Eventually, even this part of the journey became easier.

As I traveled this new and tortuous path, I realized I was learning how to maintain my health through exercise and a good diet, and to maintain my spiritual well-being through Bible study and prayer. I counseled our sixteen grandchildren according to their need and interest as appropriate and provided some resources essential to meet family needs through a stimulating and demanding work schedule. While frenetic activities brought satisfaction, nothing, including family, could fill the hole in my heart. Instead, God provided healing by teaching me new lessons that I had not fully appreciated or learned in years as a pastor and a physician/scientist.

Lessons Learned

1. After the difficult work of the acute and chronic phases of grief is over (usually one to three years), the *suddenly single* person usually realizes that life must go on. It will never be the same, there will still be turbulent swings of emotions, but new patterns emerge and new relationships are forged. Sometimes, entirely new interests appear. In my case, it was a new desire to share with others through the writing of this book.

2. Arriving at a new direction in life is painful, but imperative. The stark reality of the permanency of death is eventually accepted. Men may face many challenges in acquiring domestic skills. Women may need to acquire other skills which were typically done by their husbands. Each case is different in its details, but similar in nature.

3. Previous relationships with married couples may undergo change. One may feel out of place in the world of couples. This

is particularly true because it is unusual for a couple to be equally friendly with both the husband and wife of another couple. Old relationship patterns will inevitably change.

4. The *suddenly single* person will benefit from healthy habits of spiritual devotions, exercise, and diet.

5. There are no right paths. The work in the *Land on the Other Side of Grief* is arduous and complex. The land has mountains and valleys of uncharted experiences. Because of the many changes, the traveler needs a new compass and a new pair of glasses to navigate in this new land. The Worldview of the single person will determine in large measure the chosen path.

6. If possible, a couple should discuss their mutual goals for the life of the person who will be suddenly single. Such discussions will ease the journey in this land. *The "honey do" list continues!*

7. The greatest lesson learned was to trust God. It sounds simple but it is not! I had to learn to mute my controlling tendencies. As I endeavored to understand the puzzle of my remaining years, I realized I cannot do so. I can only rely on God's loving guidance for meaning and direction.

8. I no longer view my experience as the winter of my life, but as a new springtime in which I can celebrate my continued romance with Leanne, but in a new way. I may have new ministries to begin, experiences to share, and the privilege of helping secure the next generations of our family. The journey out of the pit of self-pity began by climbing the "Hill of Difficulty" to observe a new purposeful direction in life. Leanne provided security and supported me in my adventures during our fifty-one years of marriage. *Now I must learn how to go without her physical presence.*

9. During the proofreading of this manuscript, I realize the path on this land is neither single nor straight. There are many roads somewhat like a maze. At one point, I believe I am trusting God, but on another turn I see the vestiges of control. On this journey, I sometimes take two steps forward and one-step backward. Sometimes, it is even many steps backward!

10. Periodically, grief will suddenly reappear. Be prepared!

6

Love's Final Gift to the Suddenly Single

Dying is not at its root a medical process. It is a process with profound and obvious physical dimensions, but that is only part of it. Like other natural processes — birth, giving birth, love, making love — dying is a natural process infused with profound emotional and spiritual dimensions.[23]

Central to this chapter is one's view of death and how that understanding changes over time. In a comprehensive series of lectures, Philippe Ariè[24] uses art depicting death and customs of burial to trace the changes of society's attitude toward death from the Middle Ages to the mid-twentieth century. He notes that for many years the concept of death slowly evolved from the focus on the deathbed, where the person who was dying was in charge and orchestrated the major events, to the mid-twentieth century where death usually occurs in a hospital. Ariè writes:

> Death in a hospital is no longer the occasion of a ritual ceremony, over which the dying person presides amidst his assembled relatives and friends. Death is a technical phenomenon obtained by the cessation of care, and determined in a more or less avowed way by a decision of a doctor and the hospital team.

At the conclusion of his book, Ariè poses an interesting query: "Is there a permanent relationship between one's idea of death and one's idea of self?"[25] In this section, I posit that the answer is yes and that it is defined by one's Worldview. Accordingly, I will frame this section of the book in traditional, biblical terms in

---

[23] John Fanestil, ibid., pg. 7.

[24] Philippe Ariè, *Western Attitudes toward Death from the Middle Ages to the Present* [translated by P. M. Ranum] Johns Hopkins University Press, Baltimore and London, 1975, pg. 88-107.

[25] Ibid., pg. 106.

which life after death is by the grace of God and accomplished by faith in the death and resurrection of Christ who is the propitiation for our sin. The reality of eternal life through Christ is the underlying theme. Yes, death is a new transition to a veiled world, but confidence in the promises of Jesus gives us certainty in the face of uncertainty. Therefore, death is a logical outcome of life in this sinful world and is neither to be feared nor avoided at all costs.[26] The fourth stanza of the hymn "Oh, Love That Will Not Let Me Go" is from Romans 8:39 and summarizes this view.

> Oh Cross that liftest up my head,
> I dare not ask to fly from Thee;
> I lay in dust life's glory dead,
> And from the ground there blossoms red
> Life that shall endless be.

In an insightful book on his pastoral experiences, Pastor John Fanestil focuses on faith and a commitment of one's entire life to the will of God.[27] He begins with a description of the "happy death" of Mrs. Hunter. This concept of a happy death is mostly foreign in Western society, but I sincerely believe that Leanne, too, had a happy death.

From a slightly different perspective, Joyce Hutchinson, a nurse who works in hospice and oncology, opines,

> Being with the dying is one of the most intimate experiences on this earth. It is very much like being in the delivery room as a baby is being born, and we all know what a miracle that is. Well-being at the other end of a person's life as he or she is preparing to be born into eternal life is as great a miracle.[28]

---

[26] "For me to live is Christ and to die is gain" (Phil. 2:21).

[27] J. Fanestil. ibid., pg. 214. "By reclaiming the tradition of the happy death, we can break with the modern silence about death, and we can break it with songs of praise and thanksgiving. In the face of death we can sing with ancients that God is the beginning and the end of our lives, the very source of our being and eternal home."

[28] Joyce Hutchinson and Joyce Rupp, *May I Walk You Home? Courage and Comfort for the Caregivers of the Very Ill*, Ava Maria Press, Notre Dame, Ind. 1999, pg. 20.

Physicians have struggled with their own response to death when faced with a life-threatening condition. For example, Dr. Basta noted,

> Being suddenly presented with the possibility of your death works a brutal kind of magic. All the petty details of your life are swept aside. What matters is one small point of light ahead of you. You become fixated upon it. Call it awakening, transformation, or a road to Damascus experience—it is truly life altering. Your value system is rattled at the core. In one moment, the once infinite, invincible, indestructible, resolute, and confident person learns finitude, vulnerability helplessness, and insecurity, and yes, fear."[29]

As another example of the impact of a potentially life-threatening disease on a doctor, I described my own experience with a very atypical case of immature white blood cells in my blood during an illness after my graduation from medical school but before my internship. The differential diagnosis was between leukemia and mononucleosis. In a lecture to medical school students after becoming dean at the University of Rochester, I described the horrifying experience of being the subject of medical discussions by physicians and students.

The comments in the Rochester newspaper, The Democrat and Chronicle, described the fears that I experienced at that time. The storyline was that if the dean had his way, all young doctors would spend some time in a hospital as a patient.[30] Unquestionably, unless a physician has been confronted with a potentially deadly illness in his own life, it is difficult to understand the fear and anxiety that accompanies a diagnosis of a life-threatening disease. The hospital instead becomes a work place and the patients are

---

[29] L.L. Basta, *Life and Death on Your Own Terms*, Prometheus Books, Amherst, N.Y., 2001, pg. 12.

[30] "If Dr. Frank Young had his way; all young doctors would spend some time in a hospital — as a patient. About 25 years ago, shortly after he graduated from medical school, Young became ill. The doctors thought he might have leukemia. For a week he lay in a hospital bed. The residents—doctors in training—would come by on their rounds to listen to their instructors discussed his condition. 'it was a terrible experience,' Young said. 'Suddenly I was lying on the other side of the bed, dealing with all the insecurities and fears of a patient, listening to whatever they would conjure up for me.'" Democrat and Chronicle, April 20, 1979.

examples of disease. The science of medicine wins over the art of medicine or compassion!

There are many opinions about death. In contrast to this Christian view, Wong, et al.[31] described the existential view. They posit that death motivates people to pursue personal meaning for their lives. Fear of death is based on the failure of the individual to find meaning in one's life and death. As the person ages, the lack of accomplishment can be acquainted with failure. One has not completed the goals that were previously thought to be attainable. Fear of death can also lead to the demise of self, additional pain and suffering, poverty, and the loss of the ability to change events for the positive. Simply put, *the lack of a life well-lived.*

Gifts Given and Received During the Passing of a Loved One

Three major types of final gifts may be exchanged during the passing of a loved one provided there is sufficient time. I will illustrate this with stories. First, and most important, is the grace that God gives to each partner in the marriage. As the marriage matures, there is a special bond between the husband and wife. This bond is not experienced by anyone else in the family. Assuming the married couple has kept a hedge around their union, even the children will not know the depths of intimacy, friendship, companionship, and experiences of the parents. Although children and friends may have observed a couple from outside the hedge, only the pair knows the depth of their interaction and knowledge of each other.

Looming death will lead to an irrevocable tearing of a marital fabric that has been woven for many years. This tearing is depicted by the art on the front cover of this book. It is entitled "Overcome by Love." Dear Reader, you may wonder about the name of this art. It is to illustrate that God's love overcomes the tragic pain of death.[32] Each spouse will have a different experience of God's grace during this time of loss. Yes, both are participants in the same

---

[31] P.T.P. Wong, G.T. Reker, and Gesser, "Death Attitude Profile Revised: A Multidimensional Measure of Attitudes Toward Death." In *Death Anxiety Handbook: Research, Instrumentation and Application* [ed] Robert A. Neimeyer, Taylor & Francis Publishers, 1994, pg. 122-123.

[32] "Brothers, we do not want you to be ignorant about those who fall asleep, or to grieve like the rest of men who have no hope" (1 Thes. 4:13).

tearing of the fabric of marriage, but each will see it from a different perspective.

This grace may be so palpable that many can witness the peace and growing faith of the person who is leaving to go to be with the Lord as was the case with Leanne's passing. Such peace was also described in Mrs. Hunter's happy death. It is at times of greatest turmoil, such as the death of my father and my son's paralysis, that I felt God's presence palpably. For others, it may be a quiet sustaining faith. As noted in the poem "Footprints," God's presence may only be realized in retrospect.[33] There are many ways God's grace is experienced.

Second, there are gifts that the departing spouse gives to family and friends as a final legacy of love. Just like the memory of the first romantic kiss or the birth of the first child, these final gifts are seared into one's memory. The first and last words and actions of a person are the most significant and memorable. I used this principle in my professional life when a government colleague or a faculty member requested a meeting with me. I listened carefully to the introduction, as that was the setting for the meeting, but when the meeting was coming to an end, I paid the most attention. Inevitably, people raise the critical points at that time. Final utterances are usually the most significant.

Third, there are the gifts that family and friends give to the departing person in the last months, weeks, or days on earth. These tender expressions of love will be remembered for years. Regretfully, a significant number of people die suddenly, leaving the family to mourn without the exchange of these gifts. The next chapter will focus on practical ways gifts can be given throughout one's married life and particularly shared in the "golden years" so that one is prepared for a sudden departure from spaceship earth.

God's Gift

As one of the spouses becomes terminally ill, there is a difficult strain placed on the marriage. In these few sections, I will try to relate what I have seen in both the ministry and in medicine as a couple prepares for the most traumatic separation in life. While our own experience may or may not be representative, I hope it

---

[33] Margaret Fishback Powers, *Scripture with Reflections Inspired by the Best-Loved Poem*, Gift Books Hallmark, 2006, pg. 2.

will provide helpful insights. It is important to realize that each one of us has a time to die.[34] Unfortunately, we tend to look at death only as an enemy rather than a natural consequence of living. On a cellular level, if there was not a constant remodeling through the death of certain cells during development, a fertilized egg could not become a human being. Yet, death remains a horror to most humans.

There is an initial and predictable emotional experience following a terminal diagnosis. This experience includes anger, denial, depression, and ultimate acceptance. It is important to emphasize that God is present throughout all of these phases even though His presence may not be appreciated.

Each partner will experience God's grace differently. For some there is anger at God for the loss of a loved one. For others, there may be an overwhelming sense of depression. I have known those who have lost their faith in a just and loving God with the death of a spouse or a child. A panoply of reactions may occur. Faith, life experiences, and paths taken after the death of one's spouse usually modulate individual responses.

God's Gifts to the Dying Spouse

Helping a couple find acceptance of impending death **is** one of the most important ways a health professional or a pastor can aid a person's passage from this world to the next. This is a sensitive and complex set of discussions. It is a privilege to serve the suffering in this hour of need. In fact, the minister may play a more important role than the physician may at the moment of passing. In my experience, a gentle explanation of the options of therapy to the person and the family, including a discussion of the meaning of death and the reality of eternal life, is the most helpful approach. I have found that it is very difficult for me to enter this discussion if a person does not have a strong faith structure. Nevertheless, I have done so even if the person does not believe in God. However, under these circumstances, general discussions about faith are omitted unless I am asked a direct question. From a pastoral standpoint, I endeavor to discuss the Scriptures of

---

[34] "There is a time for everything, a season for every activity under heaven: a time to be born and a time to die, a time to plant and a time to uproot" (Eccl. 3:1-2).

comfort regarding life after death with the members of the congregation who are facing death and then medically explore options available.

In one case, after the person died, the daughter who was planning the memorial service for her father told me, "Just use the Scriptures that you shared with daddy while he was alive." Essentially, I had preached her father's memorial service to him while he was still living. I have been surprised repeatedly by the gift of peace that God gives to the person who has accepted the process of dying as a natural part of the cycle of life. On many occasions, I witnessed a transition before my very eyes as the dying person changed focus from life on earth to life in heaven.

Leanne was particularly comforted by these words from our pastor: "You are on a path not of your own choosing, but with a companion of your choice, Jesus". While she knew that she was leaving earth, God granted her a sense of real joy as she anticipated heaven. This sense of peace was so strong that she was able not only to accept her own death, but also to give counsel to members of the family and friends in matters of faith. One of her closest friends stated that she saw an angel at each corner of the bed the night before Leanne passed on. I do not know whether Leanne saw these visitors as I did not see them or learn of the observation until after Leanne had died.

Not only did Leanne experience peace, but also she was able to readily accept her limitations and even joke about them. Her sense of peace and acceptance enabled her "circle of care" to adjust to the very difficult task of helping her in the dying process at home, whether it be managing bodily functions, assisting her to turn in bed, or just being with her in these sensitive moments. We read Scripture and prayed together. This drew us closer to God. Furthermore, she was able to convey how God was comforting her at this time.

God's Gifts to the Surviving Spouse

There are a few generalizations frequently noted as a spouse copes with the death of a partner. These include anger at God, questioning the existence of a compassionate God, depression, regrets, guilt, overwhelming sorrow, pity, and loss of the will to live. Even C. S. Lewis, the eminent Christian apologist, had doubts upon his wife's death.[35] Rather than a full discussion of each of these emotions, I will relate my own experience and augment it with those of others in the hope that it may help you. Usually, one's faith, life experiences, and the path taken after the death of a spouse modulate one's reactions on this journey.

It took me a long time to realize God's gift to the *suddenly single*. Bondage by a morose self-pity snared me in a dark net for many months. It is odd that even though I knew the Scriptures of comfort[36] and used them in many funeral and memorial services, I was not at peace. I read books about heaven, about grief, about angels, about Christ's struggles with death and dying, and still, I was greatly perplexed. I knew intellectually the power of Margaret

---

[35] C. S. Lewis, ibid., pg. 17.

[36] "Do not let your hearts be troubled. Trust in God trust also in me; if it were not so, I would have told you. I am going there to prepare a place for you. And if I go and prepare a place for you, I will come back and take you to be with me that you also may be where I am. You know the way to the place where I am going" (Jn. 1:1-4).

"Jesus said to her, 'I am the resurrection and the life. He who believes in me will live, even though he dies; and whoever lives and believes in me will never die. Do you believe this?'"(Jn. 11:25).

"But Christ has indeed been raised from the dead, the first fruits of those who fall asleep. For since death came through a man, the resurrection of the dead comes through a man. For as in Adam all die, so in Christ all will be made alive" (1 Cor. 20-22).

"So it will be with the resurrection of the dead. The body that is sown is perishable, it is raised imperishable; it is sown in dishonor, it is raised in glory; it is sown in weakness, it is raised in power; it is sown a natural body, it is raised a spiritual body" (1 Cor. 15:42-44).

"Brothers, we do not want you to be ignorant about those who fall asleep, or to grieve like the rest of the men, who have no hope. We believe that Jesus died and rose again and so we believe that God will bring with Jesus those who have fallen asleep in him. According to the Lord's own word, we tell you that we who are still alive, who are left till the coming of the Lord, will certainly not precede those who have fallen asleep. For the Lord himself will come down from heaven, with a loud command, with the voice of an Archangel and with the trumpet call of God, and the dead in Christ will rise first. After that, we who are still alive and are left will be caught up together with them in the clouds to meet the Lord in the air. And so we will be with the Lord forever. Therefore encourage each other with these words" (1 Thes. 4:13-18).

Fishback Powers' poem "Footsteps."[37] Nevertheless, I remained confused. I was desperately trying to make sense of what I learned in Scripture, what I experienced in a walk of faith, and how these fit into what seemed to be an abyss of grief.

Ever so slowly, through reading and meditating on Scripture, I applied God's Word to my life. In time, I began to realize that God was always present with me! No single Scripture served as a turning point. Rather, it was the overall richness of God's Word that transformed my mind. It was not elegant sermons, though they were a comfort. Nor was it conversations with brothers in the faith, though they were of transient solace. It was reading God's Word that finally and almost cataclysmically led to a deeper understanding and peace amidst the waves of grief. Finally, as I said before, a realization stabbed my consciousness. I was attempting to control my own grief process instead of trusting God. As I realized this failure, I began to trust God to sustain my life (see "Trust God," pg. 81). Yet there were still times when I resorted to my own controlling nature, but these were becoming less frequent.

Each person will find a different seminal moment when the veil of grief begins to lift. I learned the richness of Scripture was a gift of God that could heal my soul. Similarly, Madeline L'Engle[38] noted as she compared her longer marriage to the shorter marriage of C. S. Lewis, "After a long and fulfilling marriage it is quite a different thing. Perhaps I have never felt more closely the strength of God's presence than I did during the months of my husband's dying and after his death. It did not wipe away the grief. The death of a beloved is an amputation. But when two people marry, each one has to accept that one of them will die before the other." The men in the widowers group that meets at our home similarly stated that they drew closer to God after the death of their spouses. Yet, as C. S. Lewis observed, there are times of grief where religion is of limited comfort.[39]

---

[37] Margaret Fishback Powers, ibid. Gift Books Hallmark, 2006.

[38] Madeleine L'Engle, In foreword, *A Grief Observed*, C. S. Lewis, Crosswicks, LTD, 1989, pg. 6.

[39] "Talk to me about the truth of religion and I'll gladly listen. Talk to me about the duty of religion and I'll listen submissively. But don't come talking to me about the consolation of religion or I shall suspect that you don't understand." C. S. Lewis, ibid., pg. 37.

I realized that being *suddenly single* required looking at the world differently. The process of grief creates a vibrantly colored kaleidoscope of emotional heights and depths. As I contemplated the seasons of life, I wrote the following poem.

Passage in Time: Birth to Death

Who knows when it is the time of birth?
Conception begins with a fertilized egg.
It grows and develops within the fallopian tube
And finally implants in the lush uterine valley.

You developed in darkness surrounded by water.
Organs grew until the encasing water escaped.
After development nine months later - transition time.
You were born to loving parents on April 9.

Each life is a celebration, a gift that really is divine.
You emerged after a pressure-filled journey into bright light.
A spank on the bottom, a very loud cry and sucking in air.
Life began with growth and development there.

You passed through many stages on a journey through life
Childhood, teenage years, nurses training, nursing, then wife.
Birthing your family and developing into a nurturing mother,
When four married: you became grand and great grandmother

You traveled in many moves over three score and ten.
Journeys to different locations on roads with bends,
In sickness and health, we traveled in sun and storm.
Until you passed – now I celebrate your birthday forlorn.

My love for you is intense, eternal and will never die.
We are parted on earth and I still mourn and cry
Realizing now it is not because of your change of state.
Aching for closeness to you as you completed my life.

Sitting in my chair with thoughts scattered in the air
Contemplating yesterdays and embracing our lives.
Vibrant colors within fabric, our marriage wove together,
A brilliant torn tapestry enfolding me until I die.

I know I must live on but it will never be the same.
I am comforted by knowing I will see you again.
Faith grows stronger as I groped along this path,
Jesus, my companion will walk with me till the last.

Frank, April 9, 2009

Leanne and I had a similar faith lens, but our belief was communal and I must confess that my faith and my relationship with God were modulated sometimes by my priorities and my relationship with Leanne. Now, I had to re-examine my own personal relationship with God. This exploration eventually led to a new peace. First, I had to come to grips with my own idolatry. I based the peace that emerged on a fuller understanding of my access to God.[40] This peace came when I finally realized that I was powerless[41] and only God could heal the deep wound in my heart. Essentially, I came to know God in a new and deeper way through this difficult process of understanding and working through grief.

As I look back upon this journey in the *Land on the Other Side of Grief*, I realize that there is still a long path ahead. Each day presents new challenges and experiences, but God's presence is sufficient for peace. I have learned to experience peace in the presence of separation pain.

Gifts from the Departing Spouse

Throughout your life, there are many opportunities to give gifts to your loved ones and friends. Yet, it is when you are preparing to depart from this world that people are most prepared to receive your words. The dying person can make a lasting difference in a number of ways. The first, and perhaps the most important, opportunity is to share one's faith through word and deed with those who come to visit, particularly family members. It is at this moment in life that you are most believable. Leanne most certainly lived her faith and shared it with all who came to visit her. Many said that they came to comfort Leanne, but left more comforted themselves.

Second, it is important to reconcile any conflicts, particularly within the family. Death is a one-way street. It is tragic to depart without forgiving those with whom you have a grievance or to die without reconciling differences with others.

---

[40] "Therefore since we have been justified through faith, we have peace with God through our Lord Jesus Christ, through whom we have gained access by faith into this grace in which we now stand" (Rom. 5:1-2).

[41] "You see, at just the right time, when we were still powerless, Christ died for the ungodly" (Rom. 5:6).

An example of this in my own experience was when I made a pastoral visit to a woman who was critically ill with stomach, cancer. I had the opportunity to refer her to another physician to address her cancer, but she also told me that she and her daughter had not spoken for years. She was, clearly, very troubled about this and asked me what she could do to effect reconciliation before she died. I recommended that, upon discharge from the hospital, she simply take a bouquet of flowers to her daughter's home and knock on the door. I told her that when her daughter opens the door, she should merely hand the bouquet of flowers to her and say, "I love you." Those words opened a portal to reconciliation and, in the eleven months that the woman lived, she and her daughter had a fine relationship.

Third, during the final months on earth, one can counsel children and grandchildren with regard to behavior modification, recommendations for living based on life experience, and guidance for the future. Leanne was able to share her final thoughts in at least one conversation with each child and grandchild.

In this regard, Leanne gave me three remarkable gifts. First, as described in chapter two, Leanne went shopping in her wheelchair with our daughter Peggy to buy me a Father's Day gift and card. She picked out a beautiful Lladro porcelain figurine of a young man and woman on the beach. Although she could no longer write, she picked out the card and dictated her inscription to Peggy. This card remains on my dresser so that I can look at it whenever I pass by. The figurine is carefully centered on the mantelpiece in the living room where I keep her special things.

Second, as I have said before, she lived her faith with grace and often asked, "Is it wrong to have so much joy?" I believed then, and still maintain, that she must have been able to anticipate and see heaven as she prepared to depart this earth. This was a great gift to me.

Third, we were able to discuss what I should do with the remainder of my life. It was a remarkable gift to have her guidance. It has enabled me to execute these plans for our family, our church home, and my work in accordance with what we desired to do as a couple. It gave me a map for implementing our plans during my journey in the *Land on the Other Side of Grief*.

I also observed Leanne receive and give gifts to the women in her Bible study who faithfully came over twice a week to sing hymns and to fellowship. As I write these lines, tears of gratitude come to my eyes as I think of the way Leanne shared the intimacy of her dying with family and friends. We will never forget these remarkable gifts.

Gifts to the Dying Spouse

The terminal illness of a spouse introduces many stresses and strains for which few people are prepared. Most men are much less nurturing than women. However, at the time of a life-threatening illness, a man needs to understand the needs of his wife as never before. His wife's greatest desire to be loved and cherished exists at these moments of great emotional fragility.

Most wives, although not all, will more naturally nurture and "nurse" a terminally ill husband. In spite of these differences, the panoply of emotions of the dying spouse is the same in men and women. These emotions include anger at the impending loss, depression, guilt, anxiety about unfinished agendas, and the inevitable onset of the grieving process. Amid this discordant symphony of emotional turbulence, this time together is a special opportunity to share with one's spouse the most intimate aspect of their relationship—love.

It is a gift to one's dying spouse to administer classical nursing procedures that are required as a person loses bodily functions. Couples may be forced out of necessity to engage in never before shared intimacy such as skin, bowel, and bladder care. Then too, there is a need to manage medications and master household tasks to ensure that the environment is calm and orderly to ensure the comfort and tranquility of the terminally ill spouse. This includes minimizing tension between family members. This can complicate the environment of the sick bed. Understanding and implementing the desires of a dying spouse is probably one of the more significant gifts that one can give. The threat of death brings time management into stark reality. Marital responsibility cannot be abrogated! Do not become consumed with all the mundane tasks! First and foremost, *always be a loving husband or wife to your terminally ill spouse!*

Therefore, it is important to organize the environment within the home with the circle of caring. This usually involves about ten people to aid a couple in coping with a variety of doctor visits, household chores, shopping, and social coordination. These ten may be composed of family members or friends. The critically ill person should control this caring circle for as long as possible. The caring circle frees the couple to focus on each other.

The dying spouse is usually quite concerned about the comfort and quality of life for the surviving mate. It is comforting to know that your partner will be able to live independently, carry out their common goals, ensure their legacy, and manage family affairs.

I learned that I had to be an equal partner in this journey with Leanne. We decided that I would cease all work activities outside of our home. Our sons and daughters were also able to manage many of the household duties. This allowed me to give Leanne the loving and caring attention to make her process of dying at home as comfortable as possible. This was important because she desired to remain in our home rather than a nursing home or hospice facility. I wanted to be available to provide loving support for her final journey of our married life. This will not be possible for every couple and other accommodations will need to be made. There should be no guilt about this. *Working to provide for the family is also a precious gift!*

Another gift was to respect Leanne's need to maintain her independence as long as possible. For instance, it is natural to find oneself monopolizing the time of your terminally ill spouse. I had to be careful to avoid this because Leanne needed to talk one-on-one with each of our children and grandchildren as well as with special friends. I had to realize that her needs were the ones that must be attended to, not mine. *This, too, is a great gift.*

A gift to Leanne that I might have easily overlooked was the need to manage my own stress as much as possible. I was aided in this by consultation with physicians and the use of anxiety modulating medications. I was also able to alleviate some of my stress by sharing my fears and anxieties with confidantes who were removed from our immediate environment.

Similarly, it was critical for me to be conscious of getting sufficient rest to avoid weakening my immune system. Since I had chronic heart disease, it was imperative that I not complicate her dying process with an acute illness of my own. My most important gifts to her were to provide unconditional love, support, and a comfortable environment while she was still alive. *To give her this gift, I needed to stay healthy and rested!*

So, how should a couple spend their final weeks? There is no right answer to this dilemma. In my pastoral experience, some people have chosen, if possible, to stay at home throughout their entire illness. Others have chosen to use hospice care outside of the home or a skilled nursing home. The financial situation of the family will also significantly influence this decision. However, the love required to sustain one's life-long partner is independent of finances. *Love is a priceless gift!*

I found that an unexpected process was taking place as I supported Leanne during these last few months. Her faith, courage, and ability to cope with the threat of dying, coupled with the intimacy that we shared in managing her physical limitations, caused me to fall deeper in love with her than I ever had before. This surprised me immensely because we were extraordinarily close throughout our married life. Perhaps it was because a new degree of oneness was forming as we prepared to part. *This was a gift we gave to each other!*

The final gift was being with her as she died. It is impossible to know whether she was able to hear me during her comatose final moments, but I was able to hold her and to tell her how much I loved her as she was in the very act of dying. The intimate comfort during death is love's final gift. I realize now that staying behind as my wife departed was a great gift. This gift can be given only once. I pray that each person who survives a partner's passing will be able to give that ultimate final gift!

Love's final gift is comforting one's spouse at the moment of death and remaining behind to accept the terrible burden of grief!

Lessons Learned

1. A long and loving marriage usually results in a bond that is more intimate than any other human relationship. The "till death do you part" vow in the wedding service is not appreciated until the fabric of the marriage is torn apart by the death of one of the partners. The change is irrevocable. C. S. Lewis likens the death of a spouse to a surgical operation.

> To say the patient is getting over it after an operation for appendicitis is one thing; after he's had his leg off is quite another. After that operation, either the wounded stump heels or the man dies. If it heals, the fierce, continuous pain will stop. Presently he will get back his strength and be able to stomp about on his wooden leg. He has "got over it." But he would probably have recurrent pains in the stump all of his life, and perhaps pretty bad ones; and he will always be a one legged man. There will hardly be a moment when he forgets it. Bathing, dressing, sitting down and getting up again, even lying in bed, will all be different. His whole way of life will be changed.[42]

As one passes to the *Land on the Other Side of Grief*, life will never be the same. There may be new relationships, new interests, and a closer relationship to God, but stabs of pain from the loss of a most cherished wife or husband will, inevitably and repeatedly, return. Yet, life continues in a different way.

2. God is present throughout the entire married life of a couple even though we may not perceive it palpably. God's grace can introduce the *suddenly single* to a new and deeper relationship.

3. If the couple has time to give each other gifts, these gifts will be lasting treasures. Not all couples do! The most cherished gifts are those given by the dying partner as he or she prepares to surrender life's relationships. These include the plans to complete the goals of their marriage, material gifts of pictures

---

[42] C. S. Lewis, ibid., pg. 65.

and other treasures, and most importantly, the gift of watching one's mate draw closer to God while passing into his presence.

Not everyone will experience this gift, as a partner may pass suddenly in an accident or a catastrophic terminal event. In addition, the spouse might not be there when the partner leaves. These few words are not designed to provoke guilt at being absent from the deathbed, but instead, to posit that even this scene of great sorrow may be one of intimate comfort.

4. A spouse's final gift is to hold the dying partner as death occurs, and to whisper lovingly that it is all right to leave. The change is rapid. As one's spouse dies, the warmth of life departs in a few moments. *The departing spouse is spared the heart-wrenching experience of journeying to the Land on the Other Side of Grief. The burden is yours and mine!*

5. I have concluded that a large part of my grief was due to wallowing in self-pity over my loss. The brief vision that I had of Leanne during the Christmas season of 2010 was one of immeasurable comfort. I took solace in the fact that I was not alone in such a phenomenon. C. S. Lewis also experienced a remarkable event after the death of his wife that he only vaguely described.[43]

6. Each member of the family will have a separate and distinct grief process from that of the spouse. Nevertheless, the couple can assist in the grief process during the very time of dying of a spouse before separation by death. I pondered these times and wrote the following poem.

---

[43]C. S. Lewis, ibid., pg. 86-89.

MY LOVE FOR YOU

How could I describe my love to you?
Start by telling you that you are five-foot two?
With golden hair and eyes that are sky blue,
But it wouldn't begin to do justice to you.

I've held you in my arms for over fifty-two years.
Looking into your eyes in times of sunshine and tears
I have gazed with wonderment at all that you do,
With courage, grace, compassion, and actions so true.

I could always count on you being there for me.
You gave me respect, love, and the opportunity to be free,
To engage in career battles and struggles not of your making,
Enabling our family to prosper by giving and not taking.

I admire the courage you showed from the very start.
Our marriage began with financial struggles and parting.
From your own family and your comfortable environs,
In Ohio, you began life as nurse, wife and mother, too.

You took each challenge that was thrown your way,
We moved many times: you thought in Rochester we'd stay.
The call to Washington came one day: tears for a while,
You moved to a new city and began all over with smiles.

So how would I describe my love for you?
It's impossible to say in view of all we've been through.
But I will clearly focus on the rock of our marriage.
Together with Christ in the center enabled us be true.

We have been through problems, triumphs and laughs,
But I'll remember most the moments when you passed,
From this world to the next to be in your Savior's arms,
Made whole, now safe from your cancer's harms!

Frank, January 10, 2009

7

A Life of Bonding and Maturing

How can you believe if you accept praise from one another, yet make no effort to obtain the praise that comes from the only God? —Jn. 5:44

Before discussing ways that a couple can prepare to care for a spouse with a life-threatening illness, it will be helpful to take an inventory of a bonded life. I hope that this will stimulate you to undertake an annual inventory of your marriage and to make modifications in your relationship before a catastrophic illness strikes. This overview focuses on many aspects of life that will affect your marriage at this sensitive time of transition.

The basic concepts come from pastoral counseling both with couples preparing for marriage and those facing the separation of death. There is a great difference in the joyful transition at the beginning of a marriage and horror of an anticipation of death. I hope that these few thoughts will help.

Preparation

Long before you identify a person with whom you wish to spend the rest of your life, it is important to understand your own Worldview. This includes defining your values and determining the traits that you desire most in a potential partner. Regretfully, even now, many men select a mate by moon light, and a good farmer would not pick hogs that way! The family of origin largely determines one's basic criteria for choosing a spouse, interpersonal skills, and values such as honesty, trust, conflict resolution, commitment, communication, and the understanding of each other's relationship with God.

Learning who and how one can trust results largely from early experiences with one's mother, but also with one's father, siblings and friends extending even into the teenage years. It is important that every Christian fully trusts God. While this seems simple and self-evident, it is often unappreciated as a fundamental foundation in marriage. Oz Guinness notes, "...and underneath everything lay dependency and trust."[44] A person's faith will ebb and flow. Faith does not plateau. It is either increasing or decreasing.

The core of one's self is the strength derived through one's concept of God and trust in God. All other facets surround this core. Chapter eight further illustrates a view of self. When I was dean at the University of Rochester's School of Medicine and Dentistry, I had the privilege of interviewing candidates for admission into medical school. Most students thought the dominant questions in an interview would be related to medicine. In particular, most candidates prepared to describe their interest in medicine, including their academic courses or their plans for a career in medicine. I wanted to ascertain core. I usually asked two *simple* questions: What do you dislike? What are you willing to die for? In my opinion, until one sorts through values in life and knows what one would die for, one is not prepared to live. The ethos of one's life is influenced by the answers to these questions.

Similarly, the potential partners, should, in my opinion, share the same Worldview and faith. Leanne and I symbolically taught our children this lesson through a yoke for oxen that we purchased in an antique store.

Photo 11: Leanne and Frank before the second Reagan Inaugural Ball

We hung this yoke on the fireplace to teach our children and grandchildren that it was important to be equally yoked. One of our children even took our picture in front of the yoke as we prepared to go to the 1984 inaugural ball of President Reagan.

---

[44] Oz Guinness, God in the dark: the assurance of faith beyond a shadow of a doubt, Crossway Books, Wheaton, Illinois, 1996, pg. 11.

The potential couple's method of conflict resolution is in large measure formed within their family of origin. This skill is extraordinarily important because conflict resolution is the road to understanding the other person. In pastoral counseling, I have learned that much of the discord within a marriage comes from poor skills in conflict resolution. To simplify how different people handle conflict, I will refer to four types: icers, avoiders, screamers, and negotiators.

Icers solve conflict by punishing the other person with the silent treatment. I have seen such an approach extend even to an icer's siblings and children. *Avoiders* tend to prevent conflict at all costs. This person retreats into a shell of non-confrontation. I am sure you have seen this pattern as well. *Screamers* develop a resolution similar to World War I trench warfare. They lob verbal volleys of high-pitched anger between each other. This behavior in engaged couples, is a very dangerous sign. *Negotiators* benefit most from their early family patterns. They practice the skill of give-and-take. They are most likely to succeed in getting to know the inner core of the other person's life. They also realize that resolution of conflict not only involves give-and-take, but is also an avenue to get to deepen the marriage bonds. Courtship provides an opportunity to learn how conflicts are resolved, but remember that both participants are likely to be on their best behavior.

Commitment is another essential part of one's character. Leanne and I are old fashioned in that we believed in the integrity of keeping commitments even in the midst of skirmishes and disagreements. With one transient exception, our commitment never wavered. As mentioned earlier, this occurred during a particularly stressful time when we moved from California to Rochester. We both believed that when we made our vows to each other, we were married for life. It was our job to work out our differences, not only through negotiation, but by understanding each other's frustration and stress. Leanne was married to a difficult person because I maintained a very heavy work schedule throughout our life together. We needed to be able to resolve complex schedules together based on mutual consent.

Effective communication is the hallmark of a rock solid relationship. As the couple lowers the barriers to their inner selves, there is a beautiful opportunity of knowing each other intimately. This baring of self is a kind of emotional nakedness.

Compared to this self-revelation, physical nakedness is easy. Emotional, mental, and intellectual nakedness is a process of *becoming* that lasts throughout the life of the marriage. This form of naked communication is also preparation for becoming *suddenly single*. Thus, these basic skills and patterns form the foundation of the couple's relationship. Nevertheless, separation by death or divorce will test these skills!

It is important that the couple have continual discussions to evaluate their spiritual health and goals before marriage. A critical pre-marital decision is whether or not to have a Christ-centered home. Not only does this define the early phase of the marriage, but it will continue to form the foundation after one becomes *suddenly single*. When Leanne and I taught young married couples in Sunday school, one of our favorite courses was entitled "Husbands and Wives." We believed the most important lesson in the series was the development of a spiritual action plan.

Most men and women in the workforce are used to having goals established for their job. Yet, very few married couples focus on a spiritual action plan. We admonished single young adults, college students, and married couples to develop a spiritual action plan. One key element is corporate worship, by that I mean participation in church and Sunday school. Corporate worship is only one of the fundamental components, yet it is an essential part of spiritual growth. As a pastor, I must emphasize that merely being a "Sunday-go-to-meeting Christian" misses the richness of a relationship with God. It is important to remember that we learned to love because God first loved us.[45] The spiritual action plan includes corporate worship, Bible study, and quiet time with God, as well as prayer, hymn singing and defining how one intends to live life before others.

---

[45] "Dear friends, let us love one another, for love comes from God everyone who loves has been born of God and knows God. Whoever does not love does not know God, because God is love. This is how God showed his love among us: He sent his one and only Son into the world that we might live through him. This is love: not that we loved God but that he loved us and sent his Son as an atoning sacrifice for our sins" (1 Jn. 4: 7-10).

Courtship and Marriage

Courtship is an exciting, dizzying, passionate phase of learning about each other. It is a prelude to what may be a marriage and it provides an opportunity to determine whether the potential partners are compatible with each other through the exploration of the very traits mentioned above. If one fully intends to be committed "until death do you part," this is a very important analytical process. It is, by-and-large, based on one's early family experiences and subsequent relationships during the formative and maturing years. Particularly important is the family of origin in which each was raised. Both partners bring into marriage the customs of their childhood home. These become expectations for the spouse and even the smallest things can become sources of contention in the marriage.

Let me illustrate. I admired my father-in-law for his great skills in doing tasks around the home. He laid hardwood floors, skillfully mastered carpentry, and performed all sorts of repairs. He painted the entire outside of Leanne's double story home by leaning the ladder against the side of the house. I was like my father, a person who is not particularly skilled in repairs and dreadfully afraid of heights. Shortly after we were married, Leanne asked me to wash the outside of the windows. At that time, we lived on the upper floor of a two family house.

Dutifully, I began to wash the windows just as my father did. I sat on the ledge of the windowsill, hung on for dear life, and with one hand washed the window. Leanne exclaimed, "That's not how it's done. Borrow a ladder and wash the windows from the outside." My fear prevailed and I steadfastly refused to do the job other than as my father did. Later, we lived in a different home that had three floors. One day, we returned from a trip and found all of the windows on the first two floors locked. Our house keys were inside our home. We remembered that the window on the third floor was probably unlocked. I borrowed an extension ladder and skillfully placed it firmly against the side of the house. Always the dutiful husband, I held it tightly while Leanne climbed up and entered our home through the window. I did not want her to fall. You see, by that time in our marriage, she had adapted to the fact that I was simply too scared of heights to do certain things.

Many of the little idiosyncrasies that cause problems in marriage are not discovered during courtship. Nevertheless, the couple's agreement to negotiate differences and their commitment not to let the sun set on one's wrath[46] are important principles. Throughout marriage, it is important to evaluate your spiritual health and also your marital health.

A spiritual action plan is necessary before marriage to clarify your Worldview. In our later years, we developed a pattern of morning Bible study together, followed by prayer and hymn singing. This eventually formed the bedrock of our relationship with God. In teaching young married couples, we advised that they not only review their spiritual action plan annually, but the state of their marriage as well. A reflection of the dynamics of marriage including skills of conflict resolution, balancing commitments, time management, analyzing communication skills, and parenting will serve to strengthen a marriage.

Throughout marriage, just as in your work life, your spiritual action plan, your parenting, and time management will change. No one stays on the constant plateau throughout life. Your spiritual life and the strength of your marriage will either be growing or declining. Discussions should also focus on how the other partner would live if the death of a spouse occurred unexpectedly. The consequence of marriage is the eventual dissolution of the union through an unexpected event such as death. Be prepared!

The spiritual relationship of the couple is tested in the crucible of adversity during a life-threatening illness. It will test all of their problem-solving skills, including conflict resolution, commitment, and communication. Trust and honesty will be necessary, not only between the married partners, but between the couple and the array of physicians, nurses, and family members in the circle of care. The spiritual, medical, emotional, and practical aspects of preparing to pass from this world to the next are addressed in the following chapter.

Remarriage after Becoming Suddenly Single

The early years of forming a relationship within the bonds of marriage actually build the foundation for becoming *suddenly single*. A spouse who becomes *suddenly single* after a long, intimate, and satisfying marriage usually will have a deep sense of grief and loneliness. There might even be feelings of inadequacy in

---

[46] Ephesians 4:26.

coping with the many tasks that were previously accomplished seamlessly by his wife. The need for companionship and sexual satisfaction may evoke a strong desire to bond again to another person. While there is no right answer for everyone, I would add a few notes of caution for men who desire another relationship.

First, remember that the marriage, disrupted by death, took many years to mature. Replacing a departed spouse in the midst of grief, sadness, and loneliness should be done cautiously. In such a courtship, be sure to understand the differences between one's previous partner and the new potential wife. I am not implying that it is inappropriate to bond with another. I am stating the obvious. A relationship that took many years to form is not something that is easily replaced, like "add water and mix" to make a cake batter. The essential ingredients of forming a relationship outlined above will need to be considered carefully in selecting a new partner. I have seen a number of very successful remarriages, and others that have been unmitigated disasters.

If one elects to remain single, there are many opportunities for companionship through church, social groups, and grief recovery groups. For most men of my generation, it is difficult to master the domestic skills necessary for self-sufficiency and one may develop alternate patterns for meeting these needs, from getting help with household chores, maintenance of the property through gardening services and Meals on Wheels. As mentioned previously, an example of friendship leading to remarriage is described by Susan Zonnebelt-Smeenge and Robert De Vries.[47] Their analysis of the opportunities and challenges accompanying remarriage will be very helpful to those contemplating this path in the *Land on the Other Side of Grief.*

Child Rearing

This phase of marriage is extraordinarily demanding. The foundation of relationships within the family develops here. Children inevitably influence the life of the person who becomes suddenly single. According to Dr. Paul Faulkner, "As adults, the children remain connected to the family support system, but not so

---

[47] Susan. J. Zonnebelt and Robert C. De Vries, ibid., pg. 181-216.

connected that they felt caught or entrapped. The successful families avoided the two extremes, enmeshed or disengaged."[48]

Each family has a Worldview. The Worldview influences the children's outlook and defines caring relationships. For men who become suddenly single the relationship between the father and his children is one of the most important determining factors for getting to the other side of grief. Is there a mature loving relationship between the father and his children? In large measure, this relates to the type of person the father was perceived to be as the children grew up.

In some instances, I have observed fathers who were viewed by their sons and daughters as harsh and feared disciplinarians. I have also noted cases in which the children felt abandoned such as an affair, a divorce, or a preoccupation with something beyond family. In the sad description of a dysfunctional family in a song by Harry Chapin,[49] the father was too busy to give time to his son. Subsequently, years later the son was too busy for his father. Still in other marriages, the child's spouse merely tolerates or fears the father. Of course, you can think of a wide variety of other relationships, but these interactions become the keys to the way in which the children contribute to the well-being of the *suddenly single* man.

Children can be like little video cameras on wheels. They observe and process much more by watching what the parents do rather than what they say. If one of the parents in the child's natal home has observed the mother or father take care of an ailing parent, it will markedly influence the type of relationship that the child brings into marriage and subsequently it will influence children's expectations of how they will care for their parents. For example, during WWI, Leanne's father enlisted at an early age in the Marines. During the war, he suffered severe "shell shock" or PTSD (post-traumatic stress disorder) that required multiple

---

[48] P. Faulkner, *Achieving Success Without Failing Your Family: How 30 Successful Families Achieved Family Excellence*, Howard Publishing Co., 1994, pg. 54-55.

[49] Harry Chapin, "Cats in the Cradle", "A child arrived just the other day, He came to the world in the usual way. But there were planes to catch, and bills to pay. He learned to walk while I was away. And he was talking 'fore I knew it, and as he grew, He'd say, 'I'm gonna be like you, dad. You know I'm gonna be like you.'"

hospitalizations, changed his mental health, and his capacity to hold jobs. His wife, a retired nurse, cared for him throughout their married life. As Leanne grew up in this environment, she both observed and assisted with her father's health care.

This experience made Leanne more understanding of my own time demands in medicine and in the ministry as she emulated her mother's management of the home and family. Additionally, we both had a strong commitment to taking care of our parents based on the experiences in our youth. In fact, my cousin, brother, and I were very committed to caring for our ailing parents based on family dynamics. *Nevertheless, it is neither possible nor desirable for a child to try to substitute for an intimate husband-wife relationship in marriage following the death of one of the parents. The child can be of support, but cannot replace the dead spouse.*

Mature Love and Marriage

As the children leave home and the parents rebuild their lives together, a critical time emerges in the dynamic of the married couple. There is either a deepening re-commitment of the spouses to each other or a tendency to drift apart. In fact, for love to mature, I have noted it is essential for a couple to develop new interests together. Otherwise, their marriage risks a drift in their bondedness leading to slow erosion from neglect. A yearly evaluation of the spiritual action plan and the marital health is good preventive medicine.

Leanne and I endeavored to focus on strengthening our marriage in order to minimize the impact of my career on our relationship. In fact, I accepted no new position without prayer and mutual discussion to determine the leading of God. When we approached a major turn in a career or other pathway, we would pray over a list, use the fleece approach of Gideon, or rely on providential leading. Thus, Leanne was actively involved in each of the positions that I filled and the moves we made.

As I approached sixty-five years of age and I was eligible for retirement from the Commissioned Corps, we were uncertain of our next step. Since I spent most of my professional life in universities and government, we concluded that it would be necessary to work for a few more years to ensure financial security for Leanne's later years, secure Lorrie's financial situation, and to aid in the education of our grandchildren. Yet, we yearned to have more time for ourselves. We prayed for guidance as I explored different opportunities. A local law firm offered an exceptional and lucrative position. We thought it was a possibility as the position was challenging, but not heavy lifting. Furthermore, we were interested in availing ourselves of this opportunity for excellent remuneration.

At the same time, I was invited by the nominating committee to stand for election to the Session of Fourth Presbyterian (the governing body of the church). I had been clerk of the Session two years previously and after a mandatory two-year break between appointments, I was now eligible for re-election. During the interview, I outlined my vision for the next phase of service in our church, including an integrated adult ministries program. The chairman queried whether I had sufficient time for serving again as an elder. I replied yes.

As I left the meeting, our senior pastor, Rob Norris, appeared outside the closed door of the room where the committee was meeting. He asked if I would consider being the director of adult education. I was shocked and completely unprepared for his offer. Pastor Norris and I never discussed full-time Christian service nor could he have known of my pending retirement. Furthermore, I never discussed a vision for adult ministries with him!

I told Leanne about this bombshell of an opportunity and explained the two career choices and the very different path on which each would lead us. After I finished, Leanne immediately, and in her characteristically concise decision-making fashion, said that she had been praying for a way that we could be involved in Christian service together. She believed that the opportunity in the church was the one we should take even though it would be a significant financial sacrifice. The course was clear. We embarked on this path with God's providential leading and it proved to be the greatest time of growth in our Christian walk and service. I served for six and a half years as associate pastor in adult ministries, congregational care, and as vice president of the soon-to-be-formed extension of Reformed Theological Seminary.

Our growth progressed as never before. Leanne matured through participation in an intergenerational Bible study while mine was primarily through in-depth Bible teaching in adult classes. Most importantly, we regularized our own Bible study as a couple. I regret that we did not start our Bible study much earlier in our married life, especially as I remember her hunched over her Bible studying and underlining passages. These images flash in my mind as I do my own studies now using her Bible. Her study made such an impression on me that I noted it in my letter to her as I was doing my own devotion on January 3, 2011.[50]

In addition to discussing together different career options and praying for guidance in major and minor decisions, we developed a pattern of praying for our goals the week before each year ended. In this way, we repeatedly tried to determine if we were on the correct course. We augmented this planning process through discussions while we were traveling by car. Our format was that each of us should relate three things that we like about the other person and three things that needed improvement. It was our way of continually building the bonds of our marriage.

Despite praying about and planning for many activities in our life, we did not focus on our separation by death. However, since my father and grandfather died of heart disease at a young age and I had had a coronary bypass at age sixty-nine, I did believe that I would die long before Leanne. We never considered that I would die long before Leanne would die first. Thus, like most couples, we were unprepared for the chain of events and decisions

---

[50] Here is the Scripture for today, 1 John 2:28-29. "And now dear children continue in him, so that when he appears you may be confident and unashamed before him at his coming. If you know that he is righteous, you know that everyone who does what is right has been born of him." Our quest for righteousness is one of the most important ones in our spiritual lives. In the Beatitudes, as noted in Matthew 5:6, Jesus teaches, "Blessed are those who hunger and thirst for righteousness for they will be filled." That search for righteousness and hunger for righteousness is so critical to our daily living. It is a goal where I know I fall short. As I reflect on your habit of Bible study and I could see you bent over your Bible with your little white ruler underlying Scripture as you read while I was doing other things at the table. In *Where Is God When It Hurts?* Philip Yancey cites a film by Michael Roemer in which there is a line, "People die in the way they have lived. Death becomes the expression of everything you are, you can bring to it only what you have brought to your life." You brought, in your process of dying, your unwavering faith in Jesus Christ, our Lord and Savior. By that action, you witnessed to all who came into our home. Most of all you witnessed to me. I saw your faith shine through in a way that I had never seen throughout our marriage. Thus, I fell more in love with you than ever before. In dying, you made an indelible lifelong impression in my mind and heart.

we had to make following Leanne's diagnosis of metastatic cancer. Because discussions and preparation for death and dying can reduce the stress of care giving and the magnitude of grief, the next chapter will focus on preparations that a couple can undertake prior to the diagnosis of a terminal illness and preparations to make passing from this world to the next as comfortable as possible.

Lessons Learned

1. The family imprint that each of us receives in our home is a powerful determinant of the gifts as well as burdens that we bring to marriage. These imprints have a lasting influence on the dynamics of a marriage and reappear vividly during the tearing of the fabric of a bonded life upon the death of a spouse.

2. Learn healthy habits: truthfulness, trust, conflict resolution, nurturing, and negotiation of time devoted to individual interests such as work and hobbies. Each couple's history will be different, but the habits nurtured in the early phase of marriage will carry over to one's view of death and dying.

3. Many of us make action plans for the next year or even for five years at work. Yet few of us evaluate our marriages each year and plan to strengthen our marriage systematically. This is particularly important in the childbearing years when there are so many compelling distractions. Many couples may not focus sufficient energy on the continual strengthening of their spiritual action plan and the foundation of their marriage.

4. A spiritual action plan is an essential ingredient of the couple's devotional life. Within Christian circles, there are men's Bible studies and women's Bible studies, but couples' Bible studies are less common. Family devotions may occur with children at home, but these are abandoned often when the children leave the home. Even more infrequent are consistent home Bible studies by husband and wife. We learned that devotions consisting of Bible study, hymn singing, and prayer enriched our later years of our marriage.

5. Focus on building a legacy for the next generations throughout married life. We learned it is essential to contribute to the spiritual, emotional, and financial strength of the next generation. The greatest gifts that a married couple can give to their children are their demonstrations of faithful love and devotion to each other.

6. The dynamics of the family are carried into the process of the dying of one spouse and the single life of the other.

8

Preparations for Passing

*Grief in life is a long valley, a winding valley where any bend may reveal
a totally new landscape.* —C. S. Lewis

The first encounter most married couples have with the concept
of death is in the wedding vows that unite them as man and
wife. Little, if any, pastoral counseling is given to the concept of
separation by death during the course of counseling in preparation
for marriage. Couples rarely consider that possibility when they
get married unless it is by way of a prenuptial agreement which
focuses primarily, but not exclusively, on divorce. As noted earlier,
I advise couples to take an inventory each year of their spiritual,
emotional, physical, and financial condition so that each is
prepared for an unexpected death.

Preparations during the Marriage Years

I recommend that every couple develop a general plan for the
death of one partner. This might include living wills, powers of
attorney, considerations of how to manage any potentially life-
threatening illness or injury, "do not resuscitate" orders, and
discussions of the meaning of death as well as final wishes. Such
information will form the background for decisions to be made
immediately under emotionally charged conditions. Unfortunately,
most couples avoid discussions about death and dying by
repressing such thoughts. I strongly recommend avoiding this
pitfall by carefully deciding how the surviving spouse should live
and fulfill the legacy of the marriage. *The consideration of death is
frequently a taboo subject in marriage despite the reality of its
inevitability!*

Sensitive concerns such as remarriage, sale of property
(particularly the family home), the distribution of personal effects
as an inheritance to any children, and, most importantly, the
completion of unfulfilled plans and dreams, certainly, merit careful
discussion and decisions. However, this is such a broad topic that I
shall address only points relevant to becoming *suddenly single.*

Each of us has a Worldview whether we realize it or not. It is the reference point of our understanding of self and it influences our actions either consciously or unconsciously. For people of faith, life after death is a defining concept.[51] As one matures, the essence of the self is formed and, around it, a Worldview. A person's belief, whether theistic, atheistic, or agnostic, will have a major impact on the individual's preparation for death. My Worldview was deeply influenced by my conviction that I would die early because of my family's history of cardiovascular disease.

Going into heart surgery in 2000, I was convinced that there was a significant probability that I might not survive or that I would come out with permanently impaired cognitive abilities. I spent the night following the departure of my family reviewing in my mind Scriptures that I memorize, praying for the well-being of our family and reviewing the highlights of our marriage. When the time for surgery came, I still was apprehensive about the operation but fully confident that there would be an eternity of living after death. That shared Worldview removed most of the anxiety surrounding the threat of death. I was at peace.

Figure 1 illustrates the concept of self at the center of one's Worldview and the spheres of interest, i.e., the various aspects of life. The percent of time devoted to each of the sectors will vary widely among individuals. It will also vary with the age of the spouses, the depth of spiritual life, the number of children, occupation, and recreational interests. The role of church in each family will depend on the relationship of each spouse to God. For families of faith, personal quiet time, family devotions, and Sunday school may augment family church attendance. All of these life variables make it incumbent on spouses to discuss and negotiate the actual allocation of time based on their individual interest in each of the activities in the outer circle.

---

[51] "Do not let your hearts be troubled. Trust in God; trust also in me. In my father's house are many rooms; if it were not so I would not have told you. I am going there to prepare a place for you. And if I go and prepare a place for you, I will come back and take you to be with me that you also may be where I am" (Jn. 14:1-3).

"And Jesus said to her, 'I am the resurrection and the life. He who believes in me will live even though he dies and whoever lives and believes in me will never die. Do you believe this?'" (Jn. 11: 25-26).

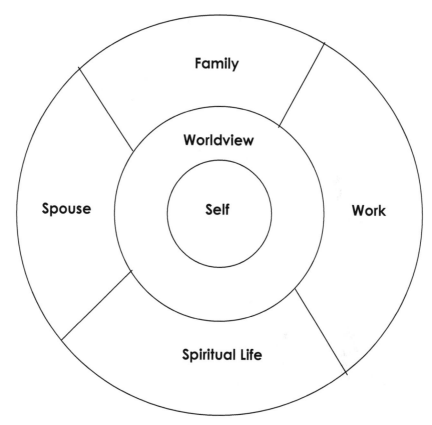

Figure 1: Spheres of Interest

Even though I taught these concepts to others, we were not fully prepared for Leanne's catastrophic diagnosis. I had even practiced what I preached, but I had planned only for my own death. We never considered the possibility that Leanne would have a life-threatening disease and die first.

Coping with a Life-Threatening Disease or Accident

At some point it might become known that one partner has a certain disease such as cancer, cardiovascular disease, neurological disorders (such as amyotrophic lateral sclerosis and multiple sclerosis), severe infections, or chronic pulmonary obstructive disease. It might also happen that one partner survives a severe accident with life-threatening complications. That partner then has a high probability of dying before the other. In Leanne's case, we received a four-to-six month warning that she would not survive her cancer. Under any of these circumstances, there is a need to make decisions that will shape the nature of the death that one experiences.

The next sections describe spiritual, medical, emotional, and practical considerations that need to be carefully, but rapidly, organized through consultation with the family, friends, and professionals. These are general approaches I use in counseling couples who are about to undergo the most traumatic event in their marriage, the death of one of the partners. Finally, there is a discussion of the factors that influence the acceptance of death by the partner who is about to experience the end of self on earth.

General Spiritual Considerations

For the Christian, the most important consideration is the intellectual and emotional assurance of salvation. It is much more difficult to handle a life-threatening situation without absolute certainty of your own or your partner's salvation. In my own case, my spiritual quest from a Sunday school faith to an adult understanding of salvation began in my pathology internship and residency. Pathology is the study of disease. It is a service that supports all other medical professions through clinical laboratory tests, autopsies, forensic pathology examinations, and research into the molecular basis of disease.

As I performed between two and four autopsies per week, I had to confront the question of whether there is eternal life after death. This was particularly pertinent to me as every day I carefully shelved and numbered mason jars containing pieces of organs and formaldehyde to ensure preservation. Is death the annihilation of self or an entrance into a new phase of existence?

I performed one autopsy on an extraordinarily wealthy individual who had been a benefactor of the university. The window in front of the autopsy table had a direct view of the building that this man donated to the university. I imagined the stark contrast between the beauty of the dedicated building and the preserved pieces of the man's organs. I visualized this lovely building being dedicated on a crisp fall day amidst the pomp and ceremony honoring the donor. It caused me to wrestle with the meaning of life and death.

Thus, at age twenty-...
resurrection of Jesus. Three
I looked at how close in time...
were to the death of Jesus. The...
the book, from about twenty to...
Jesus' death to these writings is...
events outside the government rec...
described by Paul, there were m...
appearance of Jesus after his death.

Second, I studied the change in the...
from cowardice to martyrdom. Even Scho...
belief of the disciples was genuine. Did Je...
recorded in Scripture or was there a plot in...to
faint after taking a drug and subsequently reviv...
determine whether Jesus actually died on the cr...
The Passover Plot,[53] contended that Jesus conspir...
on the cross and revived by accomplices without th...
the disciples. Further, he proposed that Jesus even...
his wounds. Schonfield posited that the person who...
Mary and by the disciples when they were fishing wa...
man. He suggested that he was the one who delivered...
and carried out the plot after Jesus succumbed to his wound...

However, studies on crucifixion lead to the conclusion...
death not only occurred, but it was due to a combination...
respiratory failure and congestive heart failure. The description...
John 19:33-35 is very consistent with either a direct cardiac...
puncture or aortic puncture which produced the blood and the...
combination of pericardial and pleural effusion to produce what
looked like water. Note that this description occurred more than a
millennia before the comprehensive description of the circulation
of blood by William Harvey in 1628. In conclusion, it is my opinion
that the type of wound described would produce sudden death.

---

[52] "For I delivered to you first of all that which I also received; that Christ died for our sins according to the Scriptures, and that he was buried, and that he rose again on the third day according to the Scriptures, and that he was seen by Cephas, then by the twelve. After that he was seen by over 500 brethren at once, of whom the greater part remain to the present, but some have fallen asleep. After that he was seen by James, then by all the apostles. Then last of all he was seen by me also, as one born out of due time" (1 Cor. 15:3-8).

[53] H.J. Schonfield, *The Passover Plot*. Bantam Books 1967, pg. 163-175.

determine whether the
...nge my life. Revelation
3:20 ...the door and knock. If
...for I will come in and dine

Third, I was intellectually comp... ...al mind, this appeared as a
faith chronicled in the Gospels ...his invitation, I realized it
3:20 challenged me, "Behold, ...This faith has strengthened
anyone hears my voice and o... ...h numerous challenging crises
with him and he with me."
clinical trial. As I emb... ...interpretation of the meaning of
eventually required a... of the surviving spouse with
over five decades as... ...nd faith of a couple, as well as that
in life. ...easure shape the interpretation of
Faith mar... ...ample, does the entire family share
one's death... ...d interpretation of death?
grief.[54][55][56]... ...e life of the spouse who is dying, as
of their... ...will color the emotional turbulence
their... ...re unresolved grievances that should be
the occur... ...ical patterns to ensure reconciliation? If
...occur, old, unresolved wounds can persist.
...rs of the family that the dying spouse has
...g their faith? In the process of dying, one's
...a crucible that to some looks like impending
...is is a most effective time for a dying spouse to
...others. In this teachable moment, the dying
...ess to family and friends in words and actions
...after death. Yet, I must hasten to add that one's

---

[54] A. Tomer and G. Eliason, Attitudes about Life and Death: Towards a Comprehensive Model of Death Anxiety, pg. 3-22 in *Death Attitudes in the Older Adult: Theories, Concepts and Applications*, [ed.] A. Tomer, Edward Brothers, Ann Arbor Michigan, 2000.

[55] A. Tomer and G. Eliason, Beliefs about Self, life, and death: Testing Aspects of a Comprehensive Model of Death Anxiety and Death Attitudes, Ibid., pg. 137-153.

[56] P.T.P. Wong, Meaning of Life and Meaning of Death in Successful Aging, Ibid., pg. 23-35.

[57] S.T. Michael, M. R. Crowther, B. Schmid and R. S. Allen, Widowhood and Spirituality: Coping Responses to Bereavement. J. Women Aging, 15:145-165, 2003.

[58] C.M. Lund, D. Ultz and B. deVries, Stress-Related Growth among the Recently Bereaved, Aging Mental Health 13:463-476, 2009.

Worldview does not vaccinate family and friends from the sorrow of grief that accompanies the passing of a loved one! The void in the family dynamic creates a "hole of pain."

The Spiritual Impact on the Spouse Who is Passing

Impending death elicits a kaleidoscope of emotion and spiritual turmoil. For possibly the first time, a person confronts the inevitable demise of the earthly self. A pastor can be of great help by accompanying the dying person through the agonal process leading to death and preparing the family for the death that will soon occur. Because the death of an individual in many ways mirrors his or her life, the surviving spouse and family can also be of great comfort if they enter into the innermost feelings of the one who is dying. This requires the dying spouse to share honestly his or her innermost feelings with others.

An understanding of the dying spouse's faith is particularly relevant in reaching decisions about continuing life by artificial means. For example, at a wedding rehearsal in our church, the father of a bride experienced a sudden dissection of the aorta. Prompt rescue and emergency surgery saved the man's life. However, in the intervening three weeks there were subsequent heart attacks and ischemic episodes in his brain and kidneys. Finally, his condition was so serious that he was maintained on dialysis and a ventilator with questionable cognitive capabilities.

As a pastor and physician, the family asked me to witness the neurological examination at the ICU and question the examining neurologists as to his prognosis. The answers I received from the neurologist made it clear that the patient's cognitive potential was extraordinarily compromised and it was highly unlikely that he would ever have any cognitive capabilities.

I administered communion to the grieving family before I delivered the findings on the medical situation. His wife was convinced that her husband had already gone to be with the Lord and that his body was merely being maintained by machines. Amid tears, and at the request of his wife, I asked the neurologist to ensure that he was free of pain. Then, I called the family members that were out of town so that they could come into town to say their goodbyes to their comatose father. At an appointed time, his wife asked the physicians to cease artificial life support measures. Within less than ten minutes, he died peacefully. Yes, grief was still there. Faith is neither a panacea nor an opiate, but the faith of the family sustained them in their decision-making.

After the immediate shock of the diagnosis of metastatic brain cancer, Leanne was truly comforted by her understanding of eternal life. Yes, she regretted that she would be leaving her loved ones, but she continued to live her life verse.[59] She repeatedly asked me and other family members, "Is it wrong to have so much joy?" Although I question my own objectivity, to the best of my knowledge, neither in medicine nor in ministry had I ever witnessed such peace in the life of a person who was dying.

In our case, Leanne's expressions of faith significantly aided us in our struggle with grief during the process and aftermath of dying. Yes, we sorely miss her! She was a person of immeasurable significance in our lives, but even in her terminal illness, she filled our memories with good counsel and love. She gave gifts of faith to each of her children and grandchildren. Leanne's love and concern for me strengthened my faith as well. In fact, Pastor Norris opined that I could not have written this book if Leanne had not requested that I start a ministry to widowers and, by extension, gave me the permission to write this book.

A Worldview defines the meaning of life and death. Thus, it serves as the lens through which the dying spouse sees and interprets the meaning of his or her death. There is ample evidence that the spiritual dimension must be considered in the dying process of a Christian. According to Grafton Eliason:

> The American Association of Pastoral Counselors (AAPC) notes that "the Gallup poll in February 1992 found that when you are confronted with a personal problem needing counseling or psychotherapy, 66% of the persons would prefer a therapist who represents spiritual values and beliefs and 81% would prefer a therapist who enables them to integrate their values and belief systems into the counseling process."[60]

Dr. M. Craig Barnes described a deathbed scene in which the dying person made a lasting impression on those in the room by her response to someone who said that it was a shame she was

---

[59] Philippians 4:6-7.
[60] G. Eliason, *Spirituality and Counseling of the Older Adult*, Ibid., pg. 241-256.

dying. According to Dr. Barnes,[61] she simply said, "What a glorious Thanksgiving. Soon, I will be with my Lord. I'm almost there."

The Impact of Death on the Surviving Spouse

Regardless of the presence or absence of the faith of the surviving spouse, the death of the partner will be a catastrophic experience. The life of a couple is over as dramatically as a sudden earthquake that destroys a building. The surviving spouse is transformed instantaneously from a "couple state" to a "single state"! I have seen some men who have become so angry at the death of a dear wife that they deeply question God's justice and love. In other cases, a spouse who does not believe in God may be dramatically influenced by the faith of his or her partner. Thus, death may be a teachable moment.

Many people are preoccupied by the pressures of life and only confront death, *the most important and inescapable part of life*, when impacted by the death of a spouse, a parent, a sibling or a child. Still others experience a period of significant spiritual growth after a Christian spouse passes from this world to the next. When one becomes *suddenly single* and is receptive to the Holy Spirit, new depths in a relationship with God may be reached. The discussions in the fellowship for widowers indicate that most of the men have become closer to God, depending on him for sustenance following the death of a spouse. This certainly happened to me. As I contemplated the dawn of New Year's Day 2011 without Leanne, I realized God was filling the hole in my life. I learned a great deal from this healing. I am ashamed I did not fully appreciate His presence earlier.

It is extremely important that the couple share in a variety of readings to provide comfort during this critical phase of life. The book *A Cup of Comfort Stories That Warm Your Heart, Lift Your*

---

[61] "Then she began to pray. She prayed for everyone around the bed: her husband, her children and her grandchildren. She even prayed for her pastor. She asked God to help me believe the words of my own sermons. Shortly after her prayer, Jean died. As we watched the lines that measured her vital signs level out on the monitor, the room was overcome by a quiet spirit. It was a sacred moment, and no one dared to defile it by trying to say something meaningful. She was passing from our hands into God's." M. Craig Barnes, *When God Interrupts: Finding New Life Through Unwanted Change*. InterVarsity Press, 1996, pg. 14.

Spirit and Enrich Your Life[62] and books about heaven, short stories, and poems are very helpful and a source of bonding for the couple. If your spouse becomes semi-comatose, remember that hearing is the last of our five senses to disappear. *A husband can read the Gospel of John to his wife and pray with her even though she may not appear to be conscious.*

If you are present in the agonizing last moments of life, please hold your spouse lovingly and whisper words of love even though there is no visible response. For example, in the last four hours of Leanne's life, she was gasping for breath and non-responsive. Yet, I held her close and told her how much I loved her. Finally, it is important for loved ones, particularly the spouse, to give the dying person permission to go from this world to the next with the assurance that all who are left behind will be all right. I did that for Leanne just before she died.

I not only experienced spiritual growth after Leanne's death, but we grew together spiritually during the three-and-a-half months of her illness through reading Scripture, prayer, and books we read for comfort. I believe that this sharing, coupled with Leanne sharing with the women from her Bible study were God's gifts to us in this most sensitive time of bonding and parting.

I recommend that you consider writing letters to your spouse. I began this form of journaling after Leanne died. After a month of profound grief, during which I could only write sporadically, I was able to write every day and I even included some pictures. Most of the letters consisted of the normal conversations that we would have. It also gave me the opportunity to tell her how much I loved her, to describe how I was managing, to discuss my feelings of grief, and to share my regrets. Eventually, when I was able to resume my devotions in the pattern we followed as a couple. I recorded and discussed the Bible verse for the day in my letters to her. Occasionally, I used a dictation program rather than typing to record a prayer or a particularly helpful hymn so that it was like talking to Leanne in a monologue with punctuation.

I also did a few other things that were very meaningful to me that have a quasi-spiritual background. For instance, when we were married, our rings were inscribed "L.T.E." (Love Through

---

[62] Colleen Sell [ed.], *A Cup of Comfort Stories That Warm Your Heart, Lift Your Spirit and Enrich Your Life*. Adams Media Corp. 2001.

Eternity). After Leanne passed, I took my wedding ring off and put it with her rings (to be passed down to a member of the family, but always kept together) and replaced it with a new wedding band inscribed, "til we meet again."

I also wear a black band underneath my undershirt that provides pressure on my right arm, which she held when we were walking. This may sound silly to some, but be creative. Discover ways to aid yourself through the acute phase of grief. You may find something that is different, but similarly important to you.

If you appreciate symbolism, use your imagination to integrate your spiritual life with meaningful symbols. The final one that I have placed in our house is a cross with a Bible in front of it opened to her life verse. There are two cups on either side of the Bible, one that is cracked and with a partially broken lip and a matching whole one. The second one will be broken when I die. These symbols take on more meaning with each passing year. I wrote the following poem on New Year's Day, 2011.

Another Year without You

On Earth, time is linear moving constantly each year.
A New Year marks a calendar with hope and fear.
Yet most remain unconscious about another sphere,
Where time is not measured as we do on Earth: right here.

You are in a different place that I only know dimly.
From Scripture, explained by Jesus in earthly symbols.
Pondering moving to 2011 not knowing what is ahead.
I do so with calm confidence, no longer with dread.

I used to worry about the state of planet Earth.
The future of our children with either tragedy or mirth,
Now I realize more fully that God is in control.
Though the future is dimly seen, I live to fulfill my role.

Since you died, I have contemplated what work is left,
In the time God granted me with vigor and breath,
To complete the tasks that I have been given to fulfill,
By yielding my life, as I endeavor to know God's will.
Frank, January 1, 2011

A New Ministry

Within the first year after Leanne's death, our senior pastor, Dr. Rob Norris, asked me to undertake a new ministry to couples faced with a fatal diagnosis for one of the partners. This was initially very painful because it necessitated reliving the events associated with Leanne's passing. This new ministry was to be an extension of my service to our congregation at Fourth Presbyterian Church. For years, I had given medical and spiritual counsel to individuals both in and out of our church. Now I would also provide emotional and practical counseling for couples during this most difficult phase their marriage.

We deal with acute illnesses all of our lives and expect to recover after a short while. Only rarely does a couple have to face the imminent death of one of the partners. The following sections summarize the kinds of decisions a couple should consider as together they face the death of one of the partners.

Practical Spiritual Considerations

Throughout the years, I have ministered to people with life-threatening diseases. Most of this counseling was in person, but some was by phone or other communication. Friends refer others to me, but usually, the ministry is to couples whom I know. When I first meet with a couple, if it is appropriate, I ask them to describe their spiritual journey. I have found that since they come to me with the knowledge that I am a pastor, this is the easiest way to enter such a sensitive counseling session.

First, I usually share with the couple some Scriptures about salvation and eternal life and then I pray. Depending on the situation, I might ask the couple to consider the spiritual legacy that they wish to leave. I have found that this is accomplished best through stories about the way Leanne and I faced this dreadful moment. By describing what Leanne and I did in the face of death, I can share my faith in a less threatening fashion.

I describe the preparation of Leanne's memorial service, deciding who would conduct it, the selection of our burial location, and the use of a prayer card as a final message. I urge that they prepare their memorial service as a last testament. As I share about how Leanne and I made these decisions, I gently inquire as to how the couple wishes to deal with each of these issues.

I also read my prayer card to them and gently suggest that the surviving spouse prepare his or hers as well. I emphasize that the prayer card is the last message that one will give to those who come to bid farewell. Perhaps I was convinced of the impact that a final testimony can have by the Session action at the First Presbyterian Church in Freeport, New York where my father was an elder. In reference to his passing, the Session minutes read, "Well done good and faithful servant. Enter now into the joy of the Lord."[63] My own prayer card includes my life verse, Romans 8:38-39, and reads as follows:

Today

Weep not that I have gone away.
Today I am home forever to stay,
In our Savior's heavenly mansion above,
And to be eternally with Leanne my love.

While on earth we had intimacy and fun.
We watched our children grow and run,
Their life's race with child rearing and care,
They nurtured me and my burdens did share.

Babes left on that August day to a better place.
For days I prayed that God's everlasting grace,
Would take her swiftly so there would be little pain,
In the full confidence that I would see her again.

What is my final message now to you?
It is that God would use you through and through.
The pleasures and pain that come your way,
Because inevitably, you will have your "Today!"

The question is whom you deem to follow in life.
Joshua asked Israel to choose whose servant they would be.
He replied, "As for me and my house we will follow thee."
Upon the answer to this question is everyone's eternity.

An example of ways in which a simple testimony can make an impact is illustrated by the last few months of a husky six-foot-two-inch sheriff in Yuma, Arizona who was married to a petite five-foot tall woman. For years, we prayed about his salvation to no avail. Pastor Smyth shared the Gospel with him when we visited him in the hospital. The man sat up and exclaimed, "Why didn't

---

[63] A contraction of Matthew 25:21.

anyone tell me that before?" After his teachable moment, he went back home and shared his newfound faith with many others.

As appropriate, I recommend that any differences the couple has with other members of the family should be reconciled. Once death occurs, these wounds may not be healed. I also explore with them what sort of spiritual support would be helpful to them during this difficult time of transition. Finally, depending on the needs of the couple, I describe my own spiritual journey and search for peach after Leanne's death. After that, I pause and wait for additional questions. I do not provide a checklist because the counseling must be customized for each couple.

Peace

This simple word is more difficult to define.
The word peace conjures up many images in my mind.
Pictures of tranquility of sunrises and sunsets.
These pastel colors do not express peace adequately yet.

Domestic tranquility is frequently described as peace.
Cessation of wars with treaties between foes.
Yet hostility belies stated peace with underlying strife.
Leading to confusion, emotional turmoil, and guarded life.

Recognizing that mortality is the common fate of mankind,
The only peace we have is not a figment of our mind.
The ultimate peace is a gift embodied by Christ himself,
Enabling reconciliation to God through His sacrifice.

Access to God is a gift beyond all measure,
It is our only lasting and eternal treasure.
Rapidly man's self-important life comes to an end.
Well done good and faithful servant is one's final amen.

Frank, August 27, 2009

Practical Medical Considerations

There are a few common points that should be considered by everyone, particularly those with life-threatening cancer. Before starting any definitive therapy, it is strongly recommend that the couple get a second opinion. Once certain therapies are initiated, other options may be ruled out. Additionally, it is preferable to be accompanied by another family member or friend so that the consultation can be clearly understood. In the emotional aftermath of the diagnosis of cancer, the couple is so distraught that it is difficult to understand the various medical options. Their minds are often preoccupied with the diagnosis, the outcome of the disease, and what it will mean to them. Therefore, another person's presence can help clarify the situation. It is particularly important that the couple go together as they will have to face all of these medical decisions jointly.

Whenever I undertake this type of counseling, I seek to help the couple frame the questions for the second opinion and I do not offer my own. If the couple has medical records, including diagnostic tests, I review these with them if they wish. If you have a physician in your congregation or a friend who is a physician, I would urge you to consider asking him or her to assist you in understanding the history of the disease, the findings of the physical examination, the meaning of the lab tests, and to explain in non-technical language the options available to you.

Particularly relevant is an understanding of the risks versus the benefits of therapy in relation to quality of life. Sometimes, the treatment may markedly reduce the individual's ability to enjoy the last phase of life, particularly in the case of cancer. These are significant decisions that must be made before therapy is initiated.

I have witnessed occasions where surgery, chemotherapy, or radiation is helpful in prolonging life and is even curative at times. However, in other circumstances, the disease has progressed so far that the treatment has limited possibilities of prolonging life. The counselor can only outline questions that the couple can raise with the health professionals and options for consideration. In addition, a great deal of information can be found on government websites. The best of these are the "Pub Meds" section at www.nlm.nih.gov and the extensive summary of the experimental clinical trials at www.clinicaltrials.gov.

In Leanne's case, consultation with the oncologists and the government sources established that only palliative total brain X-ray therapy was appropriate for reduction of the swelling, thereby reducing the need for larger doses of steroids. The radiation also might improve cognitive capability. While we were limited to steps that would keep her comfortable and improve her quality of life, it spared her the difficult side effects of therapies that would not materially alter the outcome of the advanced metastatic cancer.

Practical Emotional Considerations

A family caught in the emotional turmoil of a life-threatening disease is buffeted by a tidal wave of discordant feelings. Each family member begins a personal journey of grief after learning of the terrible diagnosis. On occasion, each person retreats into a private cocoon of concerns about how life will change. This is particularly true in the case of young children who are deeply worried about the impact of the death of a parent. The husband or wife is caught in the whirlpool of concerns for the future while at the same time attending to the needs of the dying partner. As emphasized by Callahan and Kelley,[64] the process of taking care of a dying loved one at home can be overwhelming and terrifying.

The dying person frequently prefers to be in the security of home rather than a stark hospital environment. This requires the spouse to learn how to ensure good mouth and skin care as well as managing bowel and bladder functions. Administering pain medicines may also be threatening, especially for men because the wife usually serves as practical nurse for the family.

If there are conflicts among various members of the extended family, these are likely to be magnified at this time. Therefore, it is helpful to consider involving the immediate family in decision-making and to explain future plans to them. I have noted that under some circumstances, the parents may leave one or more of the children out of the inner circle of decision-making. Under most circumstances, such action is likely to precipitate greater discord.

Accordingly, in my counseling, I ask the couple to determine as objectively as possible how to include the entire immediate family. Informing the family and reaching a consensus about the therapeutic regimen regarding treatment can avoid discordant and conflicting demands upon the health providers and arguments about the appropriateness of the course of therapy. Nevertheless, be aware that conflicts among the family members are the norm, not the exception.

In principle, the sick partner should remain in control of his or her health care and home responsibilities as long as feasible. There is a tendency for family members to try to take over prematurely, which can be threatening to the dignity of the person facing a very

---

[64] M. Callahan and P Kelley, *Final Gifts, Understanding the Special Awareness, Needs and Communications of the Dying.* Bantam Books, New York. 2008, pg. 33.

serious illness. Therefore, it is recommended that the family consider forming a "circle of care" to meet both the emotional and the personal needs of the dying partner while at the same time leaving him or her in control of tasking the various people who have volunteered to help. The dying spouse should be in control for as long as possible.

I have noted that women usually have a greater need for social support than men. This may be related to the nurturing instinct of women, although this generalization does not always hold true. If the wife has a significant circle of female friends, those friendships are likely to be very important to her. Her husband must not be jealous of the time she spends with her close friends.

In Leanne's case, she had a number of women friends within her Bible study that she had mentored. She also had led a Bible study for seventeen years. Not surprisingly, one of the younger women organized the meals that were brought to our home during Leanne's illness. Others assisted with her physical care. The Bible study women provided great emotional support for Leanne during her three-and-a-half month struggle. They came as often as once a week to sing and pray with Leanne. They were quite instrumental in sustaining Leanne's continued fellowship with her closest friends. Leanne also had other people whom she mentored and she wanted to continue to minister to them as long as possible.

Lorrie, who still lived with us, participated in the women's fellowship with Leanne. Lorrie played an important role in comforting her mother. Diseases such as cancer afford an opportunity to say goodbye to family members and to provide words of wisdom and comfort for them while they are dealing with their own grief. If the husband is deceased, female companionship is even more important, especially if the children live far away.

One is frequently immobilized by grief when the desperately ill partner can no longer take care of himself or herself effectively. It is a tremendous burden to suddenly become both caregiver and care receiver at a time when so many decisions need to be made. A family or friend can lighten the enormous emotional load of decision-making by framing the decisions that need to be made and presenting them clearly with options for solution.

For example, Jonathan said, "Dad, if you wish, I will be the Chief Operating Officer of our family. I will thereby define Mom's health needs and give you recommendations. You, as Chief

Executive Officer, can choose which one is best and we children will implement the plans." The family readily accepted this solution. Debbie and Peggy proposed ways to meet female health needs such as catheters and skin care. Frank proposed ways to make the yard beautiful. These simple thoughtful acts of love freed me to focus my attention on Leanne while the children and friends took care of many of the details. Such loving concern enabled me to fulfill my role of organizing the care of Leanne's needs by assigning tasks to be done, but also preserving my time as husband to be with my dying wife.

Each terminal illness may also be an opportunity to make memories through photographs and videos. Jonathan asked his mother if she would participate in a photographic shoot with the family. I treasure, as do our family members, the many lovely pictures that we took. Even though Leanne knew that she was dying, she provided us with a remarkable memory bank of treasured moments together with formal and informal pictures.

Leanne wanted to attend our youngest grandchild's baptism on June 15, 2008. She picked out a beautiful new dress and hat for the occasion. It was very difficult for her to get around without a wheel chair. My protective instincts notwithstanding, she insisted on going to Julia's baptism. Leanne even struggled to her feet for the moment of baptism. We took many pictures that day. Later, she wore those new clothes at the viewing after she died. I wonder if she had that purpose in mind as well.

Other Practical Considerations

The outcome of many of these practical considerations will be determined by the dynamics of the family, the home environment, the health of the supportive spouse, and the cognition, strength, and wishes of the spouse departing from this world to the next. Yet there are some extremely important practical decisions that must be discussed as soon as possible. Because most families have a division of labor, it is essential that departing spouse transfer knowledge of all his or her responsibilities to the surviving spouse.

As you anticipate a single life, it is very important to understand the unfinished dreams and desires of your spouse. Death interrupts the symphony of spousal interdependence. Therefore, I strongly recommended that you identify your common unfinished goals. Such discussions about fulfilling the couple's desires after the spouse has departed will provide a chart to help the surviving spouse maneuver through the shoals of grief. One may wish to involve the children in this planning, but it is more common that these decisions are made in the intimacy of the marriage bonds.

These discussions should include remarriage. In our case, having already decided against remarriage, we discussed ideas about how I could manage successfully. We established the list of things that we agreed I should do. Since her death, I have continued to execute this "honey do" list. These activities were very comforting, as I knew I was completing her desires. However, I must hasten to add that each couple will identify a variety of other successful strategies to help the surviving spouse cope with being *suddenly single*.

A pivotal decision is whether your beloved spouse wishes to die at home. In making such an assessment, it is important to survey the accessibility of your home and modifications that might be required. A careful analysis needs to be undertaken to ascertain whether it is realistic to enable your spouse to die in your home. If you choose this approach, you will need a circle of care to be able to relieve you of many of the daily chores, such as shopping, meal preparation, housework, and doctor visits, so that you can have sufficient time to spend with your spouse. At this stage of your married life, you will be involved with health care that you never would have anticipated. Feeding and administration of medicine is easy compared to helping with bodily functions. Bathing, toilet care, and other intimate aspects of life are usually not anticipated in the wedding ceremony when one says, "In sickness or in health."

If a spouse still works, he or she may not be able to take off all the time necessary to be the primary caregiver. Thus, other arrangements need to be made to assist in meeting the needs of the spouse. In the event that the spouse does become the primary caregiver, it is extraordinarily critical to obtain the proper amount of rest, nutrition, and support in order to avoid becoming ill and further complicating an already devastating situation. Children may spend significant time taking turns helping care for the sick parent. Many decisions that the healthy spouse and parent will face at this time of great emotional liability will be very draining.

It is critical that family members keep in mind that the focus is on the comfort of the person passing from this world to the next.

Therefore, I advise the family that it is essential to solve rapidly any disagreements and dissention. The well-being of the primary caregiver also needs to be safeguarded by family members who can observe whether healthy habits are being followed in this moment of crisis.

Similarly, it is important to consider reduction of guilt and anger that frequently plagues a family during the stress of the impending loss. Hospice may be very helpful in the terminal stage of illness, but plans should be made early enough to provide time to implement changes in the home to accommodate home hospice care. This might include moving furniture to accommodate a hospice bed on the ground floor to permit easy access.

The family may elect, or circumstances may require, that the sick person be in a hospital, a nursing home, or as a hospice inpatient unit for a long period of time. The family can explore the best way to help finance this arrangement. It is important to emphasize that there is no right choice. Each case is unique. It depends on the situation at hand coupled with family desires.

Finally, there needs to be significant discussion to determine how many people should visit and how to control the number of visitors at any one time. The desperately ill person must not be unduly taxed in this regard. This may be awkward, but it is imperative that the utmost consideration be given to the well-being and desires of the dying spouse.

The process of dying changes the relationships of all members of the family. Remember, unresolved conflicts are likely to emerge at this time. Foster reconciliation and resolve problems before anger erupts. There will be many stages in the dying process, each of which has its own set of challenges. Dominant consideration should be given to maintaining the dignity of the person who is critically ill, enabling a person to have control of his or her destiny as long as possible, and seeking guidance from professionals such as hospice, physicians, and clergy.

Whether a person will die at home, in hospice, a hospital, or a nursing home, it is critical that pain management be adequate. Maintain a supportive environment that fulfills the desires of the dying spouse. I have found that spiritual support is extraordinarily important for people of faith! Reading Scripture and favorite books, along with maintaining a tranquil setting, can be very comforting.

Lessons Learned

1. Most couples have *not* sufficiently planned for the death of one of the partners due to a cultural tendency to avoid talking about death. The emotionally charged nature of discussing death and planning for an inevitable end of life is very difficult. *Avoidance of the inevitable is the height of folly.*

2. The spiritual beliefs of the couple will significantly shape the Worldview of each spouse and define in large measure the events occurring in the process of dying. The faith of the dying spouse not only influences his or her anxiety about dying, but provides a backdrop for the formation of a legacy for the rest of the family. A dying person is most listened to when sharing the inner self and communicating final thoughts about the significance of life.

3. Even though both partners participate in the death process, each will look at death differently. The surviving spouse might perceive that the dying spouse is experiencing greater emotional suffering in the agonal phase than is actually the case. I was greatly comforted by Leanne's repeated query, "Is it wrong to have so much joy?"

4. The death of a beloved spouse will have a profound effect on the surviving spouse, even in a Christian marriage. It forces the spouse to evaluate his or her own beliefs and to try to understand the meaning of this sudden loss. Many whom I have met with have described a greater growth in their own spiritual lives after they become *suddenly single*. One widower related he now had more time for his spiritual life. This allowed him to focus on his relationship with Christ more clearly.

5. Take great care in the analysis of the risk-benefit equation to ensure that maximal quality of life accompanies prolongation of life. This analysis will be strongly influenced by the couple's Worldview and their interpretation of the significance of death. Nevertheless, the wishes of the dying spouse trump all other recommendations!

6. *Death interrupts plans and dreams.* The stress accompanying the death of a spouse and the tearing of the fabric of a long marriage will irrevocably alter the well-being of the surviving spouse. An agreement on the way the surviving spouse can fulfill the dreams that they both shared is a very healing element in the grief process.

7. There are many practical considerations to be faced when confronted by a life-threatening disease that will likely lead to death. These include the allocation of time devoted to caring for one's spouse. A determination of whether your wife or husband desires to die at home or in a hospital or other facility needs to be made early. This is a shared family decision that should include a consideration of the availability of sufficient family members to help, both physically and emotionally, to ensure proper care. There is no right answer.

   The decision will be strongly influenced by the desires of the dying spouse and the ability and willingness of the family to manage home care. If home care is contemplated, particular attention must be given to pain management and comfort care. While financial considerations are important in determining possibilities for care, love is the greatest need of the dying spouse. We all need love, especially at the two bookends of life—birth and death!

Love's final gift is remaining behind to absorb the burden of grief.

9

Legacy

The light of truth and holiness in the last stage of life should be carefully collected for the good of surviving relatives, and, when proper handed down to posterity. —John Wood[65]

As a fertilized egg develops, there is an imprinting of your entire body within the nervous system. This occurs in the mid-brain called the thalamus and some associations in the brain stem that houses vegetative functions. This neuro-matrix[66][67][68] is a "carbon copy" of your body. When a leg is amputated, there is a syndrome called phantom limb. The imprinted circuits detect a limb that is not there and can even illicit the basic biologic function of pain. As time passes, increased stimulus is necessary to evoke the pain. The sensation of pain diminishes, but always remains.[69]

Pain helps us survive by enabling us to avoid dangerous situations such as burns. Yet, in the case of an amputation, there is no limb present even though pain is perceived. Additionally, in a novel experimental approach, Gonzales was able to demonstrate discrete neurologic pathways in patients with central pain by the use of a novel tactile illusion.[70]

I suggest that a prolonged relationship could induce a process analogous to basic biologic patterning. Based on known biologic

---

[65] John Wood, In *Mrs. Hunter's Happy Death.*, John Fanestil, Doubleday, New York, 2006, pg. 35.

[66] R. Melzack and P. D. Wald, Pain Mechanisms: A New theory. Science 150:971-979, 1965.

[67] R. Melzack, Pain—An overview. ActaAnaesthesiol. Scan. 43:880-884, 1999.

[68] R. Melzack, T. J. Coderre, J. Katz, and A.L. Vaccarino, Central Neuroplasticity and Pathologic Pain. Ann. N.Y. Acad. Sci. 933:157-174, 2001.

[69] T.J. Coderre, J Katz A.L. Vaccarino and R. Melzack, Contribution of Central Neuroplasty to Pathological Pain: Review of Clinical and Experimental Evidence. Pain 52: 259-285, 1993.

[70] G.R. Gonzales, S.L. Lewis and A.L. Weaver, Mayo Clin. Proc. 76: 267-274, 2001.

neuronal patterns of memory, I propose that, in any relationship such as marriage, a person's neuronal patterning is modified in neuronal networks of the brain. This neuronal patterning is continually reinforced by the storage of memories of one's spouse throughout the intimate relationship of marriage.

When a traumatic tearing of the relationship occurs through death, the memories are still intact and a process of grief may occur that is similar to the phantom limb phenomenon. In this case, the pattern induced is the result of a long, intimate, and multifaceted relationship. As with the phantom limb syndrome, the intensity of the pain, known as grief, decreases. Over time, increased stimulus is required to evoke the pain of grief. However, the pain of grief does not disappear because the memories are internalized. *The sense of loss remains for life!*

Thus, as one moves to the *Land of the Other Side of Grief*, the grief diminishes with the realization that life must go on until one's own death. Therefore, I reasoned that I had internalized my relationship with Leanne. She remains deep within my being. Yet, the change precipitated by her death forces adaptation to a new state of life.

Whether one remarries or not, the imprint remains. According to this hypothesis, only the intensity of the pain of loss changes with time. I have found new paths on my journey in the *Land on the Other Side of Grief*, but the wife of my youth is constantly at my side as I interpret the new adventures in the light of my neural imprints. My journey continues! Life is being restored!

Note the art on the front and back covers. It was created by Martha Malana to capture a journey to the *Land on the Other Side of Grief*. The front represents the marriage after the death of a spouse. The golden face represents the living spouse and the gray face connotes the deceased spouse. The cross in the middle symbolizes the grace of God within the traumatic tear. The cross blends into the background, because the grieving spouse might not perceive Jesus' presence even though He was always there. The front cover is entitled "Overpowered by Love." *The love of God enables the grieving partner to travel in the land beyond grief to seek a new purpose for the extra time God has granted.* Each new step of understanding in the journey enables a richer restoration of this sundered fabric.

The back cover, entitled "Life Restored," depicts the final destination of the journey. The fabric of the marriage is knitted together, but the scar remains. I take comfort in the knowledge that the scars of suffering were the means by which our Lord Jesus Christ identified himself to His disciples in His resurrected body.

As I arrived in the *Land on the Other Side of Grief*, I tried to capture my feelings about my *suddenly single* life in a poem. It is my perception of the winter of my life.

Winter Dreams

Growing older my passion turns to variegated dreams,
As consciousness flows like violent rivers and streams,
Of yesteryear mixed with vivid memories galore,
And goals that we fashion building our family lore.

I can feel my body and my mind age,
It is almost like turning page by page.
Adventures shared as we embraced each other,
And blended our passions with one another.

I hold you tenderly and closely within myself.
Recalling your touch, voice, face and all else,
That made you my very special loving friend,
As I vowed to hold you to life's end.

I too will travel someday through that space.
A portal leading to a presence in God's grace.
My mind will see the image, but not your face,
As my life transmutes to a heavenly place.

I realize as I work and dream my life away,
That loves final gift to one's partner is to stay,
To ease the transition in every possible way,
Remaining behind grieving your passing that day.

As I contemplate my expected fate,
I realize that each is born and dies alone.
But I am not abandoned transitioning in space,
For Jesus has gone before to prepare a place.

Now to be with Him is my winter dream,
The glory of God and his Majesty now seems,
To occupy more of my thoughts here on Earth,
As I ponder and contemplate my spiritual fate.

Frank, January 12, 2010

"Associations" is a description of how little events and objects in daily life evoke associative remembrances of Leanne.

Associations

Our mind is a marvelous repository of events in time.
We wandered in seasons with rhythm and rhyme,
Storing memories of friends, family, and things,
Carefully hidden in neuronal happenings.

In the last few days I've suddenly discovered,
Vivid remembrances becoming uncovered,
When I saw clothing that you used to wear,
Or a picture near an unoccupied chair.

At times I see only emptiness all around,
I looked for you: you're not to be found,
Then I'll see an object lying here or there,
I realize anew how long you were here.

While wandering the aisles of the grocery store.
I pick up things each one with memories galore.
The cheese that you liked, the tomatoes for salad,
Especially the dried fruit that provided fiber.

Some of the groceries brought sad flashbacks.
Prunes prepared to hide medicinal flavor,
The commode as I help you in a personal ways,
Never thought I would love helping you those days.

I look at the furniture in the hospice bed space.
I can clearly see the cot so carefully placed,
Next to you to hold hands while falling asleep,
Portraits in jumbled relief: embraces of loving peace.

As I included pictures in letters, I review times,
Babies, toddlers, teenagers, engaged couples in lines,
Comforting me as I reflect on our journeys still not over,
Many of these associations act as a warm cover.

You encouraged me with presence by my side,
Giving security to provide for the family you bore.
Now comfortably inside I carry you around,
Vivid associations of memories that forever will abound.

Frank, January 23, 2010

You may have noticed that all poems are dated. This is because my views have changed during my travels in the *Land on the Other Side of Grief.* The journey continually refines my thinking and the meaning of the ebbing and surging of emotions. Your journey will modify your understanding of the future as well. This is the nature of the search for life and significance after a catastrophic and traumatic loss.

I began to implement our goal to leave a legacy of memories for our children and grandchildren at the beginning of 2010. On behalf of Grammy and Gramps, I gave each grandchild a replica of a brass candleholder from Colonial Williamsburg where the family vacationed for twenty years. These gifts may or may not make a lasting impression on the children and grandchildren, but they might with repetition over time.

Symbolically, the candle changes with each phase in the life of the grandchild until the last candle is gone. "The Candleholder's Tale" is included below as an example of a way for you to make written memories. Remember, the written word is much more enduring than oral traditions!

The Candleholder's Tale

Grammy and Gramps thought one day,
Long and hard for a special way,
To guide you on life's complex path,
With a lovely gift that would last.

We reasoned a special candle light,
Would illuminate your path keeping it bright,
Held by a candleholder that will never fail,
To hold your candle fast in a stormy gale.

There are many phases along the road as you grow.
Each is represented by a new candle as you go,
From infancy to toddler, through childhood and beyond,
Till you discover a special person to complete life's charm.

Then the circle of life begins a new generation.
You will light a new candle as you marvel at creation,
Of your own family unit and you will see anew,
The candle of a new light birthed by you two.

As you mature and at last grow old,
You will light a candle that is the last one to hold,
In your little brass candle holder to the very end,
Then a new Birth will begin at life's end.

Life is a torturous path of ups and downs.
The foundation of your being must be sound,
Like the candleholder representing God and kin.
Holding you steady as each new candle begins.

May God bless you as you continue to grow.
Grammy and Gramps want you to know,
God can guide the very center of your life,
Bringing you to heaven's golden light.
Grammy and Gramps, January 15, 2010

My journey in the *Land on the Other Side of Grief* continues. It is partly defined by the agreements we made on how I should live this single life. These agreements included establishing a legacy for our grandchildren through writing, helping to support their education, initiating a monthly fellowship meal for widowers in our home, creating a hospitality ministry for newly married couples in our church, and supporting our senior pastor.

Other paths were new discoveries such as writing this book and counseling couples who were about to be separated by death. Prayer, meditation, and contemplation, have resulted in a deeper relationship with God without my conscious realization that He had been sustaining me throughout this difficult journey.

I have drawn closer to God through grief. I still deeply miss Leanne, but the overwhelming feeling is no longer a deep, black sorrow, but one of gratitude. My emotions are more on the surface and I am moved more easily to tears, but the underlying sadness has diminished. I am learning to enjoy living again, but from a different perspective with the aid of a new compass and new glasses. I have a greater consciousness of the unseen world around me. I value more the unique life of every person. Most importantly, my hunger and thirst for God's Word and leading have increased.

I realize now the closeness of the unseen world. When I was younger, I did not perceive it there. Age and new "glasses" have sharpened my vision of unseen things. My faith and trust in God have grown stronger. Yes, I still have problems and I still sin. But, as Paul said, I have learned to be content.[71]

I have gained greater perspective of the totality of life. I comprehend the dark holes among the universe's bright lights. This brief poem tries to explain my understanding of the components of life within the first eight months after Leanne's death. I was still groping through the painful confusion of grief!

The Essence of One's Life

As cerebral cortical neurons connect in a tangle of dendritic tubules,
Humans interact in a meshwork of family, friendship and hostile duels,
And meanwhile the spiritual dimension of our life's ephemeral tools,
Go unnoticed in the demand of existence within earth's biologic rules.

Unless one is sensitive to nature's signs augmented by God's Word,
One is oblivious to the unseen world as feathers to the body of a bird.
One's pride can obliterate reality and lead to utter desperate folly,
Sands of time run through our hourglass without a trace on life's trolley.

Frank, April 21, 2009

I have learned that there will be many surprises as I continue my walk in this new land. Change is the only constant in life. Leanne's sudden passing has altered my life. The stark truth of her death confronts me and I am alive for a season without her. I know she would want me to carry on and to accept new God-given challenges until my journey is done. Now I celebrate her life within—two hearts beating as one.

As each of you travel in the *Land on the Other Side of Grief*, I trust you will be given a new compass and a new pair of glasses that come from a deeper relationship with God, a new wonder for the gift of life, and the ability to treasure each created being. May you receive a God-given capacity to weave a beautiful new patch in the torn fabric of life that will clothe you as you journey on in the *Land on the Other Side of Grief*, making new legacies as you reinforce old ones.

---

[71] "Not that I speak in regard to need for I have learned in whatever state I am to be content: I know how to be abased and I know how to abound. Everywhere and in all things I have learned both to be full and to be hungry, both to abound and to suffer need. I can do all things through Christ who strengthens me" (Phil. 4:11-13).

The theological symbolism and vision of the poem below is of a helmsman (me) completing his wanderings in the *Land on the Other Side of Grief* and then leaving earth for heaven. He uses a new compass and wears new glasses while roaming the *Land on the Other Side of Grief*. At long last, he embarks on his final journey into eternity.

At the fourth buoy (August 4, 2008, the day Leanne died), the boat is buffeted by the turbulent waves of grief that crashed in on my life when she died. The fading sound of the lighthouse bell symbolizes the receding earth as the wind of the Holy Spirit begins to fill the sails. The distant land is heaven, unknown and not fully comprehended, but seen by faith.

The first mate (Leanne) is not on board, but waiting in heaven. The magnet and filings represent God's creative power. The sound is in one's ears, but not in the heart of emotions or comprehension. The Holy Spirit, represented by the increasing wind, guides him. The dawn breaks after death and he arrives in heaven unharmed. Praise God!

A New Compass and a New Pair of Glasses

As I contemplate this new phase of labor,
I see a sailboat leaving a familiar harbor,
Steered by an old helmsman wearing new glasses,
Holding a shiny compass to navigate without you.

Past the fourth buoy on starboard the waves swell,
The lighthouse's loud bell is fading as he goes pell-mell,
Propelled forward as sails catch wind to skip and fly,
To a land in the distance certain yet not seen by his eye.

The first mate is missing from this unusual voyage.
To a new place only heard through ears on his face,
But drawn to it as filings of iron to a magnet do race,
Making patterns of pictures created by powerful grace.

The old man takes this journey but once on this boat.
Guided along by a forceful wind as it flies and floats,
Through the tempest, til he sees the raging sea is calm.
As a new dawn breaks: he arrives safe and unharmed.

Frank, January 15, 2011

Lessons Learned

1. Grief is a fundamental biologic phenomenon. As we travel in the *Land on the Other Side of Grief*, we travel on new pathways that are tortuous and difficult. The intensity of grief varies with the meaning of the loss. For most individuals death of a spouse or a very meaningful person is the greatest crisis of grief. Other significant losses include divorce, job loss, job change, moving, financial crisis, serious illness, deep disappointment, and broken relationships. Many of the signs and symptoms of grief are present here as well. While traveling in the *Land on the Other Side of Grief*, one is still accompanied by sorrow and loneliness but the self-centered wallowing pity is conquered by God's love.

2. Wallowing in self-pity is not a cure for grief. One must instead climb difficult mountains, work through deep valleys of disappointment, and climb new hills of difficulty. It is hard work! As I traveled in this *Land on the Other Side of Grief*, I found a new relationship with God, a deeper trust in him. I began to see His will and a new purpose for the remainder of my life.

3. My dear wife now is within my mind and heart. Our relationship and my devotion to our love continues but in a new and deeper way.

4. I have a final journey to make through turbulent seas in the ship of faith with this new compass and glasses. It is to a land revealed in Scripture—the presence of God. In the meantime, I hope to undertake a new ministry to those who are grieving and to continue solidifying the legacy of our marriage.

To God be the glory!

Epilogue

Writing this book was a journey in itself! It forced me to examine my letters to Leanne, review the poetry, and meditate on my many comments about Leanne's unexpected death and being *suddenly single*. I kept searching for a meaning for the remainder of my life. I noted that my emotions ebbed and flowed as I chronicled my travels in the *Land on the Other Side of Grief*.

I concluded the last chapter with a poem about the compass and the new pair of glasses. That poem is a description of the change one experiences after traveling through the *Land on the Other Side of Grief* and embarking on life's final journey. As I reviewed the manuscript, however, I realized that in the writing process, God had revealed to me my new purpose. How could I have missed it? I now saw signs of a new ministry — a calling to serve those who are grieving.

Now, our pastor has given me an additional ministry. He asked that as pastor emeritus, I counsel couples from a spiritual, medical, emotional, and practical standpoint when one of them is facing death. The counseling is based on my passage to the *Land on Other Side of Grief* and my study of the journey through grief.

While the shape of this new ministry is still emerging, the direction will clearly be a ministry of writing, lecturing, and counseling to prepare people to deal with the inevitable and in aiding those who are already grief stricken and *suddenly single*. I wrote the following poem, "Joy in the Midst of Pain," without fully realizing it was an outline of such a ministry.

Joy in the Midst of Pain

In the midst of grief's pain,
I would call your familiar name.
And the sound merely echoed in vain.
The lover I sought will be not seen here again!

Only much later did the truth crash through.
God had a different plan for me and you.
A new ministry appeared like a brilliant dawn,
Opening into a room to which I was drawn.

Within this room were various shades of gray
People inhabited it, not wanting to stay.
It caused them suffering, pain and wallowing pity,
Looking desperately to escape this dismal dark city.

A sign appeared stating the name of this place.
"Grief City" where people disappear without a trace,
Staying in dark recesses for a long and tedious while,
With no laughter or singing and nary a smile.

It was as if there was a loud clarion call,
To open God's Word that can dispel the pall
New perspectives of how suffering can refine faith,
Messengers might aid people through grief's wall.

Loss and pain are rules of life.
They confront us in peace and strife.
Overcoming dark clouds, fog and heavy rain,
God's peace restores: you and I can rejoice again.

Frank February 28, 2011

You, too, can find a new purpose for your *suddenly single* life. That purpose may be something you and your spouse did together or it may be a new calling. And if you are still both living, I encourage you use my "Lessons Learned" to prepare for that inevitable day. Only God can reveal to you, as he has revealed to me, the purpose of your life after you lose your spouse. However, I pray that it will be something beyond self. As you seek that purpose, consider the parable of the Good Samaritan,[72] which begins with the question, "What must I do to inherit eternal life?" Jesus asked the inquirer, "What is written in the Law?" The reply was correct. "Love the Lord your God with all your heart and with all your soul and with all your strength and with all your mind and love your neighbor as yourself." Jesus simply replied, "You have answered correctly, do this and you will live."

I can no longer hold my dear wife in a physical embrace, but she is always with me. Her passing set me on this journey of *Good Grief*. Now I must fulfill *our* legacy the best I can with God's grace. Never forget that neither your life nor mine ended with the death of our loved one. We must go on living!

---

[72] Luke 10:25-37.

Dear Friend:

I know my purpose now and I know that God has a purpose and plan for you also — I pray that this book may have helped you find it. If so, I would love to hear your story. You may contact me by email through my publisher: publisher@eleutherabooks.com.

Frank

BIBLIOGRAPHY

Bibliography

1. John Wilkinson, *The Bible and Healing*, The Handsel Press LTD, W. B. Eerdmans Publishing Co. 1998

2. Othniel J. Seiden M.D. and Jane Bilett Ph.D., *When Your Spouse Dies: A Widow and Widower's Handbook*, Thorton Publishing, 2008

3. Edward Donnelly, *Heaven and Hell*, The Banner of Truth Trust, 2001

4. Randy Alcorn, *Heaven*, Tyndale House Publishers Inc., 2004

5. Sherwin B. Nuland, *How We Die*, Vintage Books, 1995

6. Charlie Walton, *When There are no Words: Finding Your Way to Cope with Loss and Grief*, Pathfinder Publishing,1996

7. *Dignity and Dying*, [ed.] John F. Kilner, Arlene B. Miller, and Edmund D. Pellegrino, Dignity and Dying, W. B. Eerdmans Publishing Co. 1996

8. Terry Hargrave, *Strength and Courage for Caregivers: 30 Hope Filled Morning and Evening Reflections*, Zondervan, 2008

9. Mike Manson, *The Ministry of Marriage: Meditations on the Miracle*, Multnomah Publishers, Sisters, Oregon, 1995

10. M. Scott Peck, M.D. *The Road Less Traveled: A New Psychology of Love, Traditional Values and Spiritual Growth*, A Touchstone Book, New York, New York, 1985

11. Edward J. Larson and Darrell W. Amundsen, *Euthanasia and the Christian Tradition: A Different Death*, InterVarsity Press, Downers Grove, Illinois

12. Elizabeth B. Dodds, Marriage to a Difficult Man, *The Uncommon Union of Jonathan and Sarah Edwards*, Audubon Press, Laurel, MS, 2004

13. David F. Allen, MD, MPH, *Shame: The Human Nemesis*, Eleuthera Publications, 2010

14. Alastair Begg, Lasting Love: How to avoid marital failure, Moody press, Chicago, 1997

15. Alec Mother, *After Death: What Happens When You Die?*, Christian focused publications LTD, Genies House, Scotland, Great Britain, the Guernsey Press Co. LTD, 1996

16. Isaac Watts, *The World to Come*, Moody Press, 1954

17. Randy Alcorn, *50 days of Heaven* Tyndale House Publishers Inc., Carol Stream, Illinois, 2006

18. Sheldon Vann ken, *A Severe Mercy*, HarperCollins, Harper One, New York, New York 1977

19. Max Lucida, *Grace for the Moment: Inspirational Thoughts for Each Day of the Year*, Thomas Nelson Inc., exclusively for Hallmark Cards, Inc. 2001

20. C. Everett and Elizabeth Koop, *Sometimes Mountains Move*, Tyndale House Publishers Inc., Wheaton, Illinois 1979

21. Colleen Sell, [ed.] *A Cup of Comfort: Stories That Warm Your Heart, Lift You Spirit and Enrich Your Life*, Adams Media Corporation, 2001

22. Richard L. Mabry, *The Tender Scar: Life after Death of a Spouse*, Kregel Publications, Grand Rapids, Michigan, 2006

23. Michael, S.T., Crothers, M.R., Schmid B. and Allen R.S., "Widowhood and Spirituality: Coping Responses and Bereavement", J. Women Aging: 15:145-165, 2003

24. Lund, C.M. and De Vries, U. R. "Stress-Related Growth Among the Recently Bereaved", *Aging and Ment. Health*: 13:463-476, 2009

25. Schneider, D.S., Sledge, P.A., Shuchter, S.R. and Zisook, S., "Dating and Remarriage Over the First Two Years of Widowhood", *Ann Clin. Psychiatry*: 8:51-57, 1996

26. Christakis, N. A. and Iwashyna, T.J., "The Health Impact of Healthcare on Families: A Matched Cohort Study of Hospice Use by Decedents in Mortality Outcomes in Surviving Widowed Spouses", *SocSci. Med.* 57: 466-475, 2003

27. Jagger,C. and Sutton, C.J., "Death after Marital Bereavement—Is Risk Increased?" *Stat. Med.* 10:395-404, 1991

28. Hauksdóttir, A. Valdmarsdóttir, U., Fürst, C.J., Onelöv E., and Steinneck, G., "Healthcare Related Predictors of Husbands

Preparedness for Death of a Wife to Cancer—Population-Based Follow-Up", *Ann. Oncol.* 21: 354-361,2009

29. Milton, M.E. and Barron, C.R. "Spousal Bereavement Assessment: A Review of Bereavement Specific Measures", *J. Gerontol.Nurs.* 34: 34-48, 2008

30. Hauksdóttir, A. Steinneck, G., Fürst, C.J., and Valdmarsdóttir, U., "Long-Term Harm of Low Preparedness for a Wife's Death from Cancer—A Population-Based Study of Widowers 4-5 Years after the Loss", *Am. J. Epidemol.*172:389-396, 2010

31. Carr, D. "A 'Good Death' for Whom? Quality of Spouses Death and Psychological Distress among Older Widowed Persons", *J Health Soc. Behav.* 44:215-232, 2003

32. Carr, D. and Khodyakov, D. "End of Life Healthcare Planning among Young Old Adults: An Assessment of Psychosocial Influences", *J. Gerontol B PsycholSciSoc. Sci.* 62:S135-141, 2007

33. Clukey, L. "Anticipatory Mourning: Processes of Expected Loss in Palliative Care", *Int. J. PalliatNurs.* 316: 318-325, 2008

34. Wright, A.A. Keating, N.L. Balboni, T. A. Matulonis, U. A. Block, S.D. and Prigerson, H. G., "Place of Death: Correlations with Quality of Life of Patients with Cancer and Predictors of Bereaved Caregivers' Mental Health", *J. Clin. Oncol.* 28(29):4457-4464,2010

9502327R0010

Made in the USA
Charleston, SC
18 September 2011